Skippers	Area	Old Boat	New Boat
Leo Clostermans	World	Various	
Bobby Lienau	Calif. / Mex. / HI	Outaline	Good Karma
Don Tyson	World	Tyson's Pride	
Pete "Mitch" Mitchell	World	Horizons/Tyson's Pride	
Rick Defeo (Dec)	World	Tyson's Pride	
Tim Hyde	Madeira / Fla.	Tyson's Pride	
Terry Robinson	World	Tyson's Pride	
David Darrard	Stuart, Fla.		
Dider Armand	Azores	Double Header	
Stewart Campbell	Madeira / Texas	Chunda	
Charlie Johnson	Calif. / Mex.	Sea Otter	Desperate Otter
John Paul Richard	World	French Look	
James Roberts	Nomad	French Look II	
Jerry Dunnaway	World	Madam And The Hooker	
Mark Schultz	Lahaina, HI	Hinetea	
Tony Nungaray	Cabo San Lucas	Gene's Machine	
Al Bento	Honolulu, HI	Alele II	
Mark Wisch	California	Pacific Edge	
Gene Grimes (Dec)	Calif. / Mex.	Legend	
Rick Rose (Dec)	Kona /Lahaina	Big Eddy	
Steve Lassley	Calif. / Mex.	Colleen	
Julio Ansaruz	Cabo San Lucas	Various	
Lappa	Cabo San Lucas	Various	
Mike Elias	World	Ahi	Ghost Rider
Elmer Heir	California	Dorsal	
Mel Marsh	California	Atun	
R.E. Ted Naftzger	California	Hustler	48 Swordfish, Rod N Reel

WIREMEN

Scotty "Chief" Lewis	World	Various	163 To 1 Club; 573Lb / 4 Lb Test
Doug Haig	World	Various	
Rick Thistlewaite	World	Various	
Charles Perry	World	Chunda	
Gabby Gonsalves	Haleiwa, HI	Carol Joe	
Tracy Merrill	Calif. / Mex.	Various	
Willey Baxendell	Calif. / Mex.	Various	
K.C. Little	Calif. / Mex.	Various	

\# 712

TO: ERIN,

"Tight Lines, Good Times
AND Great Fishing aboard
"Lucky HATT"!
    MAY the times you have
on the new boat be as
good as the trip North!
    Go RAWERS!

                    Michael J. Elias
                    6/2/2010

Pursuit of the Grander
By Michael J. Elias

Ace Hi Publishing/Surfside

Pursuit of the Grander
By Michael J. Elias

Copyright © 2000 – Ace Hi Publishing

PO BOX 392, Surfside, California, 90743 USA

Printed in Korea

Elias, Michael J.
    Pursuit of the grander / by Michael J. Elias.
-- 1st ed.
    p. cm.
    LCCN: 00-91001
    ISBN: 0-9635355-3-6 (Cloth)

    1. Elias, Michael J. 2. Marlin fishing--
Biography. 3. Fishing.   I. Title.

SH691.B52E45 2000   799.17'78'092
                QBI00-500081

VOL. I

In football it's the Super Bowl

In baseball It's the World Series

In auto racing It's the Indy 500 (and Nascar)

In fishing its the Grander

Pursuit of the Grander

It ain't just about fishin', it's about life.

Acknowledgments vi

Preface vii

Chapter One

Jaime's Fish 2

Chapter Two

Longliners to One Liners 6

For The Record 8

Anti Perro (Cat) 10

Why M.E.? 11

Ridge Riders 12

The Amazon River 13

Belem 17

Headin' For the Corner 20

Recife 20

Woulda Shoulda Coulda 21

Silence Is Deadly 22

Islas Abrolhos 23

Vitoria 24

Chapter Three

Solid Gold 28

Key West 30

The Best 31

Chapter Four

New Year, New Boat (To Us) 34

Catalina 34

The Coves 36

Striper Tournaments 37

Chapter Five

Vernski 42

Cabo San Lucas 42

Panama 46

Comets Please! 46

King Ka-Chammie-Chammie 47

Aloha 48

Lahaina 49

The Sin Twisters 50

Party's Over 52

Chapter Six

HELLO! Back To the Present 54

Lahaina '93, A World Tournament Record 54

Chapter Seven

A Rio Return 68

Changes 68

A Rio Bummer 68

What's on The "Horizons" 69

Which Two Items? 69

A First 70

Fish oil and water 73

A Lahaina Return 1994 73

The Christmas 73

Back to the Boat Shop 74

Starting With A Bang 74

Chapter Eight

Desperado Days 76

Club De Atun O Quatro Amigos 80

On To Mazatlan 83

It Didn't Ixtapa Us From Going! 87

Cleanliness Is Next To Godliness 89

Coast To Coast 95

Chapter Nine

Madeira 98

Across The Pond 98

Azore Arrival 102

Last Leg to Madeira 105

"Tyson's Pride" 108

On The Road Again 114

Chapter Ten

Home Sweet Home! 118

Church Mouse '95 118

The Masters, Gold Cup and Classic 121

Chapter Eleven

Madeira Madness 124

Splitting Up Your Engineer 124

Shelby's Record 126

One Big Fish 128

Back Across the Pond 128

Australia's Great Barrier Reef (The Land of Oz) 129

Finish With A Flurry 132

Club Nautico 134

Chapter Twelve

Into The Thick of It 136

A Day Off! Let's Go Fishin'! 136

A Tonner? A Giant? A Monster? 146

Epilogue 148

About the Author 151

Glossary 152

Acknowledgments

For
George Elias

Linda Elias

Al Bento

and

all that have had the dream.

Picture Credits

Cover – Free Swinning 900 lb Black Marlin off Australia, Guy Harvey

Overboard sequence, Dick Harrison

Jamies fish, Unknown

Pablo Amorim's fish, unknown

Church Mouse weigh-in, Island Photo

86 Lahaina Jackpot, Donnell A. Tate

Cormorants fish, Donnell A. Tate

Marlin on its side, Madeira, Charles Perry

Church Mouse winning weigh-in, Island Photo

Shelby's fish, unknown

Black Marlin, Charles Perry

Marlin on Skip Loader, unknown

Marlin going away from boat, Charles Perry

Back cover, "Madeira Blue", Guy Harvey

Other pictures by the author

Design by Vicki Schmidt

Desktop Services by The Print Network
www.theprintnetwork.com

Preface

A lot of people have accomplished their dreams.

A lot more have not.

Big game fishing has only been possible as we know it due to the vast amounts of modern technology that has occurred in the last century. To fight a large marlin or swordfish a hundred years ago was unheard of. Many fortunes have been invested and many have committed their lives to the attempt to fight the large marlin of the world. The list of fishermen that have angled a Grander (any marlin weighing over a thousand pounds) is not very long but is very distinguished.

Chapter 1

Jaime's Fish

reg Edwards had the wire in his hand as the huge, lit-up, black marlin jumped from the port to the starboard side of the transom. This marlin was well over a thousand pounds and had just realized it was hooked. Gaffman Andrew Vinnicombe would probably only get one shot to set the gaff as the giant fish went by before Greg would have to let the wire go. If Andrew missed, Jaime would have to try to fight the fish back to the boat for another attempt to wire it. This could take a while since the fish had been hooked up only seventeen minutes at this point.

The "Cervantes" had fished the waters off of the Great Barrier Reef of Australia for many years with the experienced crew of Captain Geoff Ferguson, wireman Greg Edwards and gaffman Andrew Vinnicombe aboard. Jaime Harrison's father, knowing how much Jaime loved fishing, had decided to take the two of them down to the "Reef" from their home in Southern California to fish for the black marlin located there. Of course a Grander would be the ultimate catch of their trip.

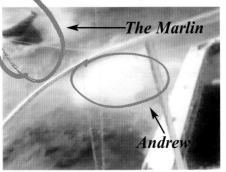

←——— *The Marlin*

Andrew

Andrew made a lunge at the big marlin with the twenty-three- inch reinforced flying gaff, but missed. He immediately stretched out over the side for the fish again and this time he sank the gaff into the shoulder of the fish. Andrew had not noticed the gaff tail line looped on the deck. As he sank the

gaff into the fish he also didn't notice his left foot inside the loop of the gaff line, going from the hawse pipe on the covering board, around his left ankle, then over the side to the gaff in the marlin. Andrew held on to the gaff line, and as he felt the 3/8" line around his ankle slip up to the top of his leg, he realized he was in trouble. He tightened his grip until the line burned his hands. As the line tightened it quickly cut into his leg crushing everything but not breaking any bones. At the same moment he was torn off of the back of the boat from the force of the eleven hundred pound black marlin and thrown into the water. As he was pulled off the boat his body spun in the air like a rag doll, from the gaff line straightening out and becoming tight. This did free his leg. Captain Ferguson jumped down from the bridge and was now at the corner of the cockpit where Andrew had been only a second before. As Andrew surfaced he grabbed the gaff line, which was extended over his head. At the same instant the great marlin jumped and straightened out the reinforced gaff, freeing itself. Within seconds Captain Ferguson pulled Andrew back onboard the boat. Andrew was in shock, sitting on the cockpit deck with his left leg bleeding. Captain Ferguson asked him if he was all right. Stunned, he replied that he was "O.K."

Meanwhile Jaime was still fighting the marlin. After forty-seven minutes, with Greg and Andrew's help, she landed the fish. They hooked up a block and tackle to bring the great fish aboard and as soon as the marlin was on deck they were off to Lizard Island to weigh in the fish and to get Andrew to a doctor.

After arriving at Lizard Island the fish was hoisted on the scale and weighed in at 1,102 pounds, it was the first grander of the season and would eventually be the IGFA's second largest fish of the year in 1985.

Jaime was ecstatic and had every right to be, she had accomplished on her first trip to the reef what many had tried for years to do. They hooked up with only an hour and a half to go on the last day they were to be there. As Captain Ferguson said, "She is one hell of a lady!"

Ashore, Andrew tried to make like his leg didn't hurt. However, since he could barely walk, the leg was wrapped, elevated, and he was given pain medication to try and make him more comfortable. The next morning he was flown to the hospital in Cairns where he had x-rays taken. They found that the area where the line tightened around his leg had crushed almost everything. The doctor couldn't believe his bones were not broken!

Remarkably, this was actually the second time Andrew had been pulled off a boat by a gaff line in a big marlin, and survived! Marlin fishing can be dangerous.

Dick & Jaime Harrison and the Cervantes Crew

Chapter 2

Longliners to One Liners

ecife, Brazil: November 1992. This leg of the trip from Puerto Rico to Brazil did not have many momentas de brilliance. The two boats had been badly battered since we left Belem, Brazil, the port at the southern entrance of the Amazon River. Evening had fallen as we entered Recife harbor and headed up the inside of the breakwater for our prearranged mooring site at one of the wharfs. As is usual and customary the mothership would berth first and after she was secure the gameboat would take her place on the outside, like a duckling behind her mom. Soon both vessels were secure. The electrical umbilical cord was connected so electric power could be transferred to "Pride" from "Horizons." "Pride" could now shut down her generator.

"Horizons" (Mom) is a 96 foot steel tuna boat design converted to a yacht, or as close as possible to one, considering her lines are definitely fish-boat quality. The exterior may not look like much but the roomy interior is spectacular. From the woodwork to the inlaid border of the custom Fabrica carpet coupled with the original oil paintings, the interior is very well appointed. She does her job serving as a mini mart, hotel, restaurant, fuel dock, repair barge, and occasional towboat. There are not many yachts around that have an original Remington bronze sculpture arbitrarily being used as a sunglasses holder. The only thing wrong with "Horizons" is that out of the dozen or so boats built to her lines, over half of them have flipped over and were lost. This is the reason for the added seventy-five thousand pounds of ballast in her keel. She carries over twenty-five thousand gallons of diesel fuel and has a very advanced centrifuge fuel filtering system. The crews never have to worry about how clean the fuel is no matter where in the world they might be fishing.

"Tyson's Pride," the gameboat, is a magnificent 62 foot Merritt sportfisher. Built of wood in Pompano Beach, Florida, she not only looks like a fine piano, she plays like one. That is when she does what she was built to do, FISH. Merritt has been building successful sportfishers for many years. Her lines showed their expertise. Her hull is sleek with a good bow and low aft to allow the wire man access to the fish that are being angled. The interior is finer than most homes, the joinery work perfect, with a finish to match. I'm sure the Merritt family is very proud of their product. Even with two twenty kilowatt generators, a full tower and all of the gear and equipment to travel any place in the world she is fast. Thirty five knots in the blink of an eye, and capable of half that on a back down if needed.

"Pride" carries a crew of four. Captain Rick Defeo, his wife Donna who organized both boats and handled a lot of the business, also two mates Terry Robinson and Richie Barrett. Rick and Donna, in their mid thirties, have been with the Tyson Program for the past five years, occasionally seeing their home in south Florida where they have a great number of trees and plants, their "other" hobby. Rick and Donna were involved in the start of the two-boat program. They have been running gameboats all over the world from such remote places as Bali to the busy coast of the eastern seaboard. Terry and Rick are from the northeast and have handled the big bluefin in the north and the blue marlin in the Caribbean, a lot of experience for that cockpit team in their mid twenties.

Peter "Mitch" Mitchell, the Australian Captain of "Horizons," is an old friend. He's from Mackay, Queensland, Australia on the East Coast, south of the Great Barrier Reef. He and I have done thirty odd thousand miles together on different vessels in the last fifteen years. Mitch always looks as though he hasn't eaten in weeks. You'd wonder if it were windy if he'd blow off the boat. Definitely a health nut (at 135 lbs.). The only disagreement we'd ever had was when he'd tried to get me to taste that axle grease he likes on his toast, veggimite! Most zeppos don't care for it either! He had called to see if I could be of assistance on this trip, so . . .

Our spot on the pier in Recife was behind two new and very large foreign longliners that were tied one in front of the other. With a contingency of Brazilian Ejercito (army) standing guard and the lack of any crew aboard either vessel, it all appeared a bit strange. Our local shipping agent had been waiting for us at the pier upon our arrival. After a brief introduction, he explained the situation regarding the vessels in front of us.

These two longliners had been working inside the fishing boundaries of the Brazilian coast. This was not a problem due to an agreement between the two countries (Brazil and an island country in the Far East). The problem, however, was that during a customary search at sea by the Brazilian Navy the fish holds on both ships were found to abound with billfish, which was a violation of the agreement between the two countries. "Friggin' Wankers!" as an Aussie Captain friend of mine would say. After

7

discovering this barbaric assassination against nature the good ol' Brazilian Navy invited the two longliners to visit the port of Recife, Brazil, under armed escort, of course. Once in Recife the process became simple: arrest the crews, fine the two ships and remove the cargo, to be dispersed in the local areas for consumption. That's what happened, but it went farther than that. The crews were arrested and after their government paid fines of over a million dollars (U.S. currency) they were escorted to the airport under armed guard, and deported. The fish were distributed to the local population. The agreement between the two countries was immediately canceled. As we found out a few days after our departure for Vitoria, Brazil, the two longliners were towed out to sea and destroyed by the Brazilian Navy. Friggin' great end to a very unhappy story.

For The Record

We are on our way to Vitoria, Brazil to fish for blue marlin. The Atlantic blue marlin record had been set February 29, 1992 by Brazilian Paulo Amorim on his sportfisher "Duda Mares." Using a Penn STW 80-wide with 130-pound mono (monofilament line) his marlin weighed in at 636 kilos (1,402 pounds). His fishing club, Iate Clube do Espirito Santo, was so impressed that they had a special awards ceremony for his achievement and presented him with a new car! The license read "1,000." Our boats' mission: try to set a new record and have fun fishing.

Both boats departed for Brazil from Puerto Rico on October 21, 1992. I was unable to join the program until the Island of Grenada. My flight via New York and Puerto Rico to Grenada was less than exciting, especially when the flight attendant said she was out of rum. It was gracious of the Cuban government to build such a nice runway in Grenada. It was a comfort knowing it was much longer than needed.

When I arrived the boats were side-tied and "Horizons" was well secured with her 1000-pound bow anchor out. Mitch said the trip down to Grenada from Puerto Rico was as easy as it gets for the two boats. They had fairly flat seas and light wind. The scenery in Grenada was as tropical as you might ever imagine, lush green vegetation, palm trees, warm water and sunny skies. The northeast trade winds combine with the humidity to keep the temperature at a pleasant level.

8

636 kilos (1,402 pounds)

Late in the afternoon a group of us went ashore. Rick, Donna, Mitch, Terry and myself headed for the harbor. Over dinner we laid out the final game plan for the balance of the trip south. The total distance from Puerto Rico to Vitoria, Brazil is 3,540 nautical miles. The trip from Grenada (600 miles shorter) should take 29 days, including stops.

Hoby

Anti Perro (Cat)

The next morning we were up early and would be underway after a short trip to the veterinarian. No, we didn't have to take Mitch in for his distemper shots. "Horizons" had acquired two butterscotch kittens and it was necessary to have them checked out and given health certificates for international travel. The older kitten was mellower than the younger kitten. Donna named the bigger kitten "Hoby," as in Hobie Cat (Catamarans), and the Australian Captain of "Horizons" named the little terror "Little Bloke." The cats were like night and day. Hoby was real happy inside "Horizons" and Li'l Bloke always wanted out; she could usually be found sleeping on top of the large coils of tow line under the skiff.

"Little Bloke"

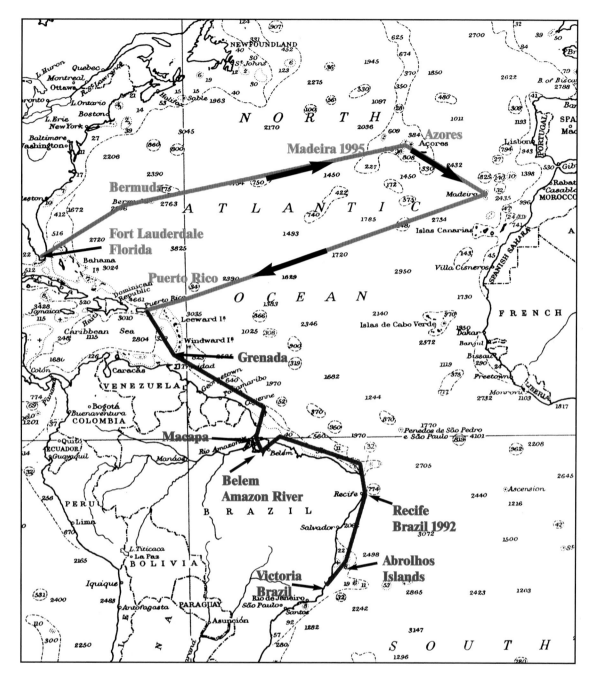

Why M.E.?

"Horizons" can stay in one anchorage for long periods of time being a "mother ship," infact the crew's sea time gets rusty and it takes a few days to get with the program after each departure on long trips. Normally "Horizons" carries a cook, engineer, deck hand, steward and Captain. When underway she carries a backup Captain/first mate and also a second engineer. My job was the backup Captain/first mate and navigator, basically back up for Mitch.

Conditions for the first few days were fine. As you travel further south from the Caribbean to Vitoria, Brazil, not only are you going against the equatorial current (that eventually becomes the Gulf Stream in the north) but also the prevailing wind is in your face. Both the equatorial current and the sea breeze are going in a northerly direction from the "corner" of Brazil north and in a southerly direction from there south. This means that we will probably get our ass kicked all the way to Recife. Once we make Recife we will be on a down hill slide to Vitoria, 27 percent of the total distance from Puerto Rico.

The sea conditions were one reason for the trip into the northern entrance of the Amazon River and out of the southern entrance. This side trip would save us two hundred miles at sea and would give us a four hundred mile run in the head waters of the Amazon River, and a chance to angle for the infamous dreaded piranha. Can you imagine angling a five-pound fish on fifty-pound wire leader and getting "bit off"? And none of that "man overboard" stuff!

Ridge Riders

As "Horizons" plowed southward on a rhumbline course "Pride" would head off during the day and fish the ridge (steep underwater drop-off). "Horizons" cruised at eight and a half knots and of course "Pride" could do whatever she wanted to. This was like the tortoise and the hare with the gameboat able to cover a lot more miles than the mothership.

They didn't even have to bring in their riggers!

We'd rather be lucky than good and that's exactly why "Horizons" released a billfish before the "Pride." I'm sure the boys on the gameboat were just "stuck" about that! The fishing for us was good on this leg. We also caught a couple of mahi-mahi and a nice yellowfin tuna.

About every three days, conditions permitting, "Pride" would rendezvous with us. We'd take her in tow and drop back a fuel line and fill'er up.

The Amazon River

Our first port since departing Grenada would be Macapa, sixty miles up the northern entrance of the Amazon River.

The Amazon River, being the second longest river in the world, is huge. You travel for one

Water color change 60 miles from land

hundred miles in the ocean heading for the entrance in sixty feet of water, or less, with no land in sight. The shallow waters are due to the millions of tons of sediment that flow out of the river mouth each year. Two-thirds of Brazil drains to the Atlantic Ocean via the Amazon River basin. The river is navigable by ocean going vessels all the way to Iquitos, Peru, 2,300 miles inland from the river mouth.

Captain Mitch & Little Bloke

Landfall was made at 16:15 hours. It was dark at 18:45 hours, we finally anchored at 19:30 hours. We decided to anchor in a bend of the river rather than run at night due to the excessive amount of natural debris (trees, etc.) on the river.

The following day after a four-hour run we arrived at Macapa. With a cheer from both crews, we crossed over the equator as we approached the town. As the boats moved through the river waters, the tide changes could make or ruin your day. With the floodtide coming in and this being the dry season, you could go all day before you would see a tide change. This was fabulous for fuel economy when the GPS (Global Positioning System) would read that the boats were traveling five knots faster than their normal speed. Sure glad we were not going in the other direction (down stream), although we would be as soon as we departed for the southern entrance.

Macapa, although not a big city, was bustling like a new town in the old west of the United States. A few hours were spent doing entry papers and picking up a river pilot needed for the five-day trip through the headwaters to Belem, Brazil, the city at the southern entrance of the Amazon River. Soon we departed and headed off for adventures unknown.

Each night when we anchored, the pilot would find an offshoot from the main river. Since there was so much traffic on the river around the clock we would be safe there.

Huge barges, ships, pongas and anything else that floats are used for transportation on this river. With all the vegetation and swamplands of the jungle, the river is THE only road. Every night we side-tied and prepared for the onslaught of bugs.

Small river boat & huts on the bank

Because this was the dry season, there were none, except huge moths that were devoured by the cats! We couldn't believe it! The evenings were actually cool, the dampness in the jungle combined with a slight breeze would quickly cool off the temperature.

The first night we were all alone. The next day as we headed along the river we would see huts on stilts with a dugout (canoe) at each one, (a car in every driveway). As we moved along the river, dugouts would paddle out to meet us, mostly children with their hands held out for anything. Both boats

River life

had a supply of candy on board but not enough for everyone. We tossed them every extra thing we could find in the next couple days as we traveled the river.

"Horizons" led the way and "Pride" followed. This was part of the game plan as "Pride" had expensive new props and we did not want any thing to happen to them. Any debris in the water would be spotted and relayed to the "Pride." It must have been quite a sight to see a sportfisher with a full tower coming down the Amazon River. The local people must have thought that was one heck of a TV antenna! At any sizeable village where a generator would be found, there was always a satellite dish!

One day we anchored at a lumber mill operated by a company in Louisiana. The Americans running the operation invited us ashore and off we went. Nice set up. They showed us their replanting program, and gave us a tour through their local rain forest. Rick and Donna went crazy over the rain forest. They have a large number of different types of trees at their home in Florida. After a few hours it was time to hit the trail. Off to the water balloon fight, "Horizons" won.

"Pride" started a water balloon fight with the mothership and found out why they have waterproof hatches. "Horizons" battened down their hatches, turned on their fire fighting pump and soon "Pride" was waving the white flag. We anchored a little while later in a secluded area and in less than an hour we were surrounded by a group of dugout canoes, with hands out. High fives weren't what these local natives were looking for.

Everyone watched for other signs of life. Besides seeing a multitude of different birds, the closest we would come to seeing the Brazilian Woolly Monkey, found generally from the central to upper Amazon basin, would be Mitch up on the radar mast.

As we cruised through the river, the two cats would stick their heads out and sniff at all the different scents in the air. I do believe they actually were enjoying the smooth conditions, especially Hoby who seemed to be a bit under the weather on the passage from Grenada. Even "Li'l Bloke" wanted inside on that part of the trip.

Belem

On our fourth day from Macapa we arrived at the city of Belem, on the Para River, the southern entrance of the Amazon River basin. Belem, a city, yes, but more of a city than we had expected. This place was BIG! There were tall buildings, taxis, crime, everything but friggin' Superman. Belem is not only the capital of the state of Para but is also one of the most attractive cities in South America. Our program meandered into the port after zigzagging through quite a maze of islands, buoys and miscellaneous BS the last few miles. It was like going twenty miles to do two. We finally arrived at the wharf in Belem, Brazil. Anyway we got there. It was a river trip I will never forget, another learning experience. The only thing missing was fishing for piranha. Our only chance was at the lumber mill but we couldn't wait until the next day to go with the guides. That's the problem with schedules.

We did our side-tie program and soon were thinking of a little shore leave. Our agent here said that it was very dangerous in this town. He obviously had never seen the wrong end of an AK-47 in downtown anywhere USA. "So don't wear your watch at night, don't be alone at night!" That's usually why crews, that have been on a boat for a couple weeks go out at night, NOT TO BE ALONE, (they have been alone too long). After all was well and done as far as the docking program, we had a cocktail and time to realize how bad this wharf really was, no rats, more like mountain goats with moustaches. It had been a long time since the boats were tied to a dock and after dinner everyone hit the hay.

Lots to do when the sun came up. We organized a refueling schedule. This meant centrifuging fuel through our system until "Pride" was full and then ordering fuel for

"Horizons" through our agent. Our agent was a representative of the fueling agency we contracted with in England. We would fax our itinerary to England and they would take it from there, arranging fuel and stores for all major stops. This saved the program thousands of dollars in the long run. We didn't know this would take almost a week to finally accomplish. Also at Belem we needed to replenish our food stores which was not as much of a problem, but a problem it was. First off, our male chef, whom had never been anywhere out of the USA, shows up on deck ready to go shopping in flowered shorts, sandals and a pink tank top. We all looked at him, it took a few minutes to decide whether or not to let him be fed to the wolves, but no one else really wanted to cook. We explained to "Hazel" that when in a unfamiliar port one usually wears long pants, a normal shirt and shoes just so you are not a target.

We had been told there was a great open-air produce market on the waterfront so we were off to the market early. All was well until some stupid kid tried to pickpocket our second engineer, a six-foot-three, 240-pound, easy-going, Mexican senior named Amadeo. Amadeo, in his late thirties, lives in Jacumba, California near the Mexican border with his wife and two children. He has worked for the Tyson program for the last fifteen years. This kid almost died when Amadeo turned around as quick as Chuck Norris and grabbed his arm. Amadeo, being the nice guy that he is, did not break his arm into little splinters. He picked him up a foot off the ground and smiled at him! Amadeo has a thick long black moustache that makes him appear to be right out of the movie "Treasure of the Sierra Madre." Amadeo can look like one mean bandito. Anyway he grabbed his wallet back from this guy and slowly put him down. The kid looked as though he had just met his maker. By that time the immediate crowd was gaping at what had happened and the local federalies were there to protect the kid from any further harm from senior Amadeo.

After a day of many tasks, both crews had dinner aboard "Horizons" and decided on who could go ashore and who would stay for dock watch. The younger guys went ashore first so maybe they'd be a little mellower for the next day or so. So off to the "circus" they went. To get off the dock you had to pass through a guard gate. When the boys returned they found that the guard had changed. Mitch, I mean CAPTAIN Mitch, being the good guy that he is, gladly got out of his first dead sleep in three weeks to

18

vouch for the semi-conscious what-in-the-hell-did-I-do-last-night crew. All I know is when daylight came there was a message at the guard gate for one of the fishing mates on "Pride." Not to mention any name, a crew member's "fiancé" was awaiting. He looked at us, just smiled and said, "What a great problem." Off he went to the guard

gate and a few minutes later he showed up with a very nice and attractive young lady who became his steady for a long time to come. They were still an item when I finally departed Vitoria for California.

A few days later Evandro Coser arrived from Vitoria, Brazil. His family has diverse businesses all over the country. Evandro had met Rick Defeo and Don Tyson a couple of years ago when they flew down to Vitoria to fish. Evandro is a great guy, he had flown to Belem to check on one of his cattle ranches near there and to go with us, as a guest, to Vitoria and especially to fish the "Pride" on part of the remaining trip.

We finally departed Belem on the morning of our seventh day. Our early departure was not to elude possible future family ties with our crew and some citizens of Belem, but to get out to sea by dark. The pace was slow with the current against us most of the way out of the river. We finally hit the Atlantic at sunset. Just before dark the boats went through an awesome display of Mother Nature. There was a current line that had waves of four feet, located in a narrow cut just before the ocean. This looked a lot worse than it was. To run that channel at night would have been nerve racking, at least for the first time.

Headin' For the Corner

Ah! The salt air, the salt water, the seas, the wind, all IN YOUR FACE, it's so special to be back at sea! One of the complaints with "Horizons" is the bridge location, in the front 15 percent of the boat. After departing the Amazon we were almost immediately in ten-foot seas with the wind at 25 knots dead center from where we were going. When in the bridge you felt as though you were airborne half of the time. The funny thing is, during the day "Pride" was next to us for this leg of the trip to Recife. They handled the seas much better than we did. They have videotape of our bow thruster being out of the water by five feet on several waves. These pleasant conditions lasted for the entire trip to the corner of Brazil, six days. As we rounded the corner the conditions almost immediately subsided. This leg found all of us doing galley duty since chef "Hazel" was a bit under the weather. When we finally arrived in Recife it was a welcome sight.

Recife

Aside from the problem with the longliners, Recife had a lot to offer, a large city much like Palermo, Sicily. After the docking drill we met the ships agent, the officials and all their friends. Time flies when you are doing official paper work on board a yacht in this country, especially after the officials have a beer or scotch. Once the legalities were completed it was very late and everyone on both boats hit the sack.

First order of business was to order fuel, we did not need the fuel but Mitch did not want to ballast the empty fuel tanks with seawater unless he absolutely had to do so. Every time we were in a port he had decided to top off the fuel. The day was busy with ordering this and that and we found things happened here a lot faster than in Belem. The fuel would be delivered in the morning. The food stores were to be delivered the next afternoon. That evening Evandro had invited Mitch, Rick, Donna and myself out for dinner. We accepted immediately. The rest of the crew was divided up so some could go ashore at night and the remainder would be on dock watch; the younger, single group was let out the first night.

Evandro has an inland ranch producing hearts of palm, pigs and chickens or a combination of the above. It took me a while to understand his Portuguese/English and my lack of Portuguese did not help. At first I thought Bon Dia (good day) meant bum day, oh well a little time and the language became easier, like every where else in the world. The restaurant we went to was amazing. It was a castle. The place even had a draw bridge and moat. The menu and wine list were world class. Did we have a feast, I'm sure glad we took a cab back to the boats.

In a couple of days we departed for Vitoria. On the way we would be stopping at the Abrolhos Islands. The conditions were excellent. Smooth, clear and the current was going our way.

Woulda Shoulda Coulda

Evandro traveled the leg from Belem to Recife with us on "Horizons." He would be traveling with "Pride" from Recife to Vitoria. Since the conditions looked to be better on this leg they'd be fishing the whole way. We departed in the morning and put the boat on a rhumbline course for the Abrolhos Islands. "Pride" headed out to the ridge to get her lines wet for the first time since before we entered the Amazon River.

Rick knew that Evandro had done a lot of fishing in Brazil and figured the boys in the cockpit would go over procedures with him, just to be safe, in case they hooked up on a big fish. Evandro had set the twenty pound test line record, catching a 170 lb 10 oz white marlin on 12/8/79. Riggers out, lines wet, four 130 Penn Internationals with all new 130-pound test line and 500-pound test leaders. The tag team in the cockpit, Richie and Terry were ready. In less than an hour they approached the ridge and altered their course to follow it to the south.

By now it was time for lunch and Donna was whippin' up a little grub for the boys when the right rigger (looking aft) almost snapped in half, it had been a while since the riggers were out and the rigger clip was a bit tight. Instantly, Terry who had been watching the lures yelled, "Might be a slob!" (big marlin). While that Rupp rigger was whipping like

21

a trout rod the reel started to zip, and instantly the line started to smoke off the reel. As Richie told Evandro to grab the rig out of the covering board (top of flat area between the hull and cockpit) Terry was getting to the first of the other rigs to bring them in. Rick by instinct put the starboard throttle all the way forward, turned the helm hard to port and then put the port throttle all the way forward. It took quite a few moments to get the boat to plane and pointed in the right direction to have this fish quartered to port. As the boat gained speed Richie yelled to Rick that they were half spooled. "Pride" WAS a match for this fish. Rick later told us that he almost got up to full throttle before they were able to stop the line from going out.

In the next three hours the fish never jumped although he was near the surface a few times. Rick had worked the boat hard assisting the angler in gaining on the fish. After all this time the fish was close. Rick had spun the boat around the fish the last couple times it had sounded. Apparently he had confused the fish, who seemed to be tiring. As they gained on the line the fish was only 50 yards from the boat but he was straight down. Evandro was beat but he was hanging in there.

The fish started to come up, Rick anticipated a shot at getting a gaff into him as Richie and Terry were already set with two rigged flying gaffs. As all this was happening, Rick saw Evandro, out of the corner of his eye, as he locked the drag all the way down. Before Rick could open his mouth to tell Evandro to set the drag back where it was the fish made a death run, the 130-pound test line snapped.

Silence Is Deadly

Rick knew the fish was well over the thousand-pound barrier. They would never know if it was or if it was not a possible record. It took Rick a while to talk and longer to talk to Evandro. When Rick called us on the SSB radio we could tell things had not gone well. The last thing he said to us that day was, "There is no excuse to ever break off any fish on a 130." A program that has millions of dollars invested in a fishing trip can't have mistakes. The slightest error can kill your chances at catching any large fish.

Islas Abrolhos

In two days we arrived at the group of islands that are a national park in Brazil. "Pride" released a good number of blue marlin on this leg of the trip but nothing like that first fish.

The islands are small rolling hill shapes and fairly barren. We anchored at Isla Santa Barbara. The marine biologists on the island doing research met us when we anchored. As we were preparing to jump in for a swim they told us that a park ranger had drown the day before. Since they had not yet recovered the body they asked if we would keep an eye out for him. (Yeah, or what might have possibly eaten him).

Later that night "Horizons" departed for Vitoria, two hundred miles to the south. "Pride" would depart in the morning. At her cruising speed she would meet us in the harbor at the same time we arrived in the early afternoon.

These two boats would be in Brazil for a year and a half and while there they missed the 50-pound ladies blue marlin record by just a few pounds. One of the biggest fish they would have on was the marlin lost off of Recife the first day they fished Brazil.

Islas Abrolhos

Vitoria

The two boats anchored off of the yacht club in Vitoria, Brazil

Vitoria is a beautiful and busy port city. When we arrived, the count on the number of ships at anchor waiting to berth was 22.

Evandro had some bad news upon his arrival home. One of his neighbors' sons had been kidnapped while walking home from school. A ransom of almost a million U.S. dollars was the demand, it was paid and he had been returned unharmed. I asked Evandro about paying such a high ransom. He responded that the people were wealthy who lived on his island and it would be a disaster to notify the police. Anyway the family had their son back and now all the fathers would make a plan to find the kidnappers. He said that it was very simple, they would pay more than the ransom if need be to find the kidnappers and deal with them accordingly.

The boats spent a lot of time in this area of Brazil and had a lot of fish on but never did land the grander. They were actually spooled a couple of times on the smaller rigs (eighties and fifties), but not the big rigs. There were a couple of anxious anglers who caused lines to break by overdoing the drags. The fish were there but they didn't get the big one.

A week after we arrived in Vitoria, after being royally welcomed by all the members of the Vitoria Yacht Club, Evandro threw a magnificent arrival party for us at his home on the island out in the bay. I arranged to head back to California. We had a couple refits scheduled at my shop. On November 30, 1992 I flew to Miami, then to southern California.

Chapter 3

Solid Gold

To fly to California from Vitoria took a bit of work. First I flew to Rio and had a seven-hour layover at Rio International, so I grabbed a taxi and arranged a three-hour tour of the city. We hit all the normal spots of interest and also checked out a couple of the marinas. They were quite large and full of local yachts. Copa Cabana Beach was filled with people even though it was late in the afternoon. Rio is quite a place but it's not for me, I fell asleep on the way back to the airport.

All flights from Rio depart for Miami around midnight, but the good news is you arrive in Miami early in the morning. On the way back to California I had a couple errands to run. I had a GPS navigation system from Paulo Amorim's boat in Brazil that needed to be dropped off at a repair facility in Miami. I also wanted to visit a couple of boat yards in Palm Beach before flying out of Miami to California.

The aftermath of Hurricane Andrew was something else. There were no hotel rooms available in the area of Miami International due to all the insurance adjusters booking up the place. The destruction was amazing. There were boats in vacant lots just lying on their sides everywhere. The devastation was obvious all the way to Ft. Lauderdale. I visited one boat yard and sitting in the yard was a beautiful 90-foot motor yacht that looked to be in good shape. Upon closer inspection I found that from the water line down there was no boat! It looked as though it had been drug down the freeway and the bottom ground off until the boat was sitting on its lines. Having been at sea in two separate hurricanes, just looking around at all the damage made my blood chill, the force a storm like that has... it is unimaginable and impossible to describe. All I can tell someone who has not been in a hurricane, "Get ready... when you're ready, get the lipstick out, apply neatly to your rear end and kiss your ass good-bye, and if you're real lucky you'll get to wipe off the lipstick!"

By the time I arrived in Ft. Lauderdale it was late afternoon. I grabbed a hotel room on the beach. Early December is a slow time in Ft. Lauderdale. The clerk at the hotel said it would pick up right after Christmas.

Back a few years ago a good friend Scott Guenther had built a new sportfisher, a Viking 57 named "Desperado." He had hired Mitch, another friend, Scotty Lewis "Vernski" and myself to deliver the boat from New Jersey to California via the Panama Canal. The trip to Florida was smooth and quick. We made the twelve hundred mile run from New Jersey to Palm Beach, Florida in three days, running at thirty knots in daylight only. The boat was to be detailed and the outfitting to be finished in Palm Beach at the Rybovich boat yard. The boat was tied up for a few weeks so I returned home during the detailing. Upon my return to the boat, now at Pier sixty-six in Ft. Lauderdale, I was instantly whisked away to dinner by a small army of the owner's friends.

After dinner we arrived at an entertainment facility known as Solid Gold, lots of beautiful ladies and not much in the clothing department. I've always told my wife that when I quit looking she'd better worry, so look we did. These friends of the owner all had companies that were multimillion dollar businesses. After a few minutes these guys had every girl in the place standing on one of the long bars and they were slipping hundred-dollar bills under the ladies' garters, which  was about all they were wearing. Vernski, Mitch and I were not on the front line for this act. In fact Vern looked at me and said that this had been going on all week. They reportedly dropped almost twenty grand into garter belts in just a few days! I looked at Mitch and Vern, then said, "And these guys give us a hard time about our bills!"

The next day as Mitch, Vern and myself were stocking the boat for our trip to California via the Panama Canal, Scott and his amigos were off investigating other Ft. Lauderdale "businesses." We called the hotel at Pier sixty-six Marina for a room service lunch on board the "Desperado." A short while later the room service cart pulled up and after the waiter set the table with linen the three of us had lunch. It was less than one of the bills under one of the garters the other night!

Key West

Bula, Pat Farrah, Jimmy Buffett, Mike Volpe, Scott Guenther, Hank Libby, Pete Mitchell, Kevin Jaffe, Dan Tsujioka & Mike Elias

Two days after the episode at Solid Gold we all took off for Key West on board the "Desperado," there were ten of us aboard. The conditions were smooth, except for a squall that rained on us for a half an hour. Scott (the owner) was getting harassed from all sides. His buddies were giving him hell over everything including being a new boat owner. I guess they just wanted to rattle his cage but the most razzing was over the fact we were going to be in Key West by one o'clock p.m.! They told him he was really full of it and there was no way we would be there until dark. Well being a bit experienced with navigation I announced we not only would be there at one o'clock but our ETA would be ten minutes ahead of schedule. They roared and laughed. At twelve-fifty we were at the Key West entrance buoy. They couldn't believe it! A little while later we were tied up in a marina in Key West.

That afternoon the boys took off for Jimmy Buffett's Margaritaville Store. The last time these guys were in town they broke the record for buying the most merchandise ever sold to one customer. They were off to break their old record. When they set this new record (especially in extra large), they asked the manager if Jimmy was in town. Sure enough he was. The manager made a phone call and arranged for the group to have lunch with him the next day. The next day we all had a bite to eat at Buffett's restaurant and met him in the process. During the meeting we had a group photo taken with Jimmy holding a hundred-dollar bill, of course.

The Best

I have a boat shop in California and I wanted to visit the Rybovich boat yard and the Merritt yard after the flight from Rio to Florida. When you do something with someone that is more talented than yourself, you may learn something. So I was off to investigate two of the best. The Rybo yard was in the middle of a huge overhaul, I found that they had merged with Spencer boat works next door. One boat that I wanted to see was in the water at the yard's slips. "Breathless" was exactly that, one beautiful Rybovich day boat about fifty feet in length, full tower, a real showpiece.

A while later I met yacht Captain/Merritt Yacht Broker Jack Ferguson at the Merritt facility. Jack showed me around the place. They were in the middle of building three sixty-five footers. One was skippered by well known Captain Bobby Brown. The story was that they were eventually going to take it to Hawaii on her own bottom. One of the original 37-foot Merritts called "Finest Kind," (not the same boat from Lahaina, Maui), had been sold and was in the yard. Her new name was "Live Wire" and her new owner was having her totally refitted. That would take about a year. The quality of the work being completed here was very impressive.

Chapter 4

New Year, New Boat (To Us)

While the Tyson boats fished the waters of Brazil, I headed home. With work keeping my nose jammed to the grind stone at my boat shop in southern California, I was barely able to make one trip to Mexico during the spring of '93. I bought a used Phoenix 27 with twin diesels, tower, Rupp riggers, nice size fishing cockpit, and a big enough interior for overnight trips. Between getting the boat operational and the shop, time was flying by. My wife, Linda, and I ran the boat over to Catalina Island for a little R & R a good number of times before the marlin season started to kick in.

Catalina

Catalina is a great place to spend the summer. Great weather, lots of coves to investigate and some fun striped marlin fishing. The stripers are caught in a variety of ways. Some anglers like to just troll lures and that can usually get some zips (strikes), hook-ups and even a few fish are landed or preferably released this way. Other anglers will troll lures (with hooks) or teasers (without hooks) and have a live bait ready to drop back as soon as there is a fish in the jigs (bait and switch). Still other people will do both, also having other crew constantly looking for feeders, sleepers, tailers, birds over fish, and of course the elusive two finner (swordfish). It is most effective to have a bow bait tank for casting. Casting off the bow is the most fun way of hooking up. This of course occurs after a fish has been spotted on the surface. The angler will go to the bow, the Captain will try to give the angler a boat position so he is casting from a two o'clock position to a ten o'clock position, using the bow as high noon and casting down wind if possible. The way a group of sleepers can "lightup" and race each other for the bait is a show in itself! The marlin "lightup" and turn an iridescent bright blue when they get excited. Of course lots of anglers will slow troll, soak a bait or even use down riggers, all of which can be productive depending on the given situation.

Of the two towns on the island, Avalon is the main one. Avalon, nestled in among the hills of Avalon Bay, has been the subject of many an artist and photographer, with the beautiful Casino standing as a well known landmark on the west side of the bay. When the fishing is slow we always liked going to Avalon, having dinner and going to the movie at the Casino Theater. Construction on the Casino started in February 1928, and was completed on May 25, 1929, fifteen months later, quite an accomplishment! The Casino was officially dedicated and opened on May 29, 1929. The theater is under the Casino Ballroom. It has to be one of the oldest and most beautiful movie theaters still open in the world today. The giant pipe organ is played forty-five minutes before the first showing, which makes quite a show in itself. The Casino is best known for the Big Bands that played in the Casino Ballroom from the time it was built and still play there on special occasions. With the name "Casino" you would think it would be a gambling Casino, but not so! It has never been used for that purpose. The 300-degree view of the bay and ocean from the walkway around the ballroom is magnificent. "Twenty-six miles across the sea, the island of romance" is a line out of an old song that has brought many couples to Avalon who returned home "families to be!" The summers here are always very busy with all the yachts, excursion boats, shore boats and express boats. This at times makes the harbor a madhouse.

The green pier stands alone in the middle of the bay. This is where you can find Rosie's fish stand, under the Harbor Masters office. Rosie's is where anglers can weigh in their fish, as Rosie is a certified IGFA weighmaster.

Also in the bay one can find the Avalon Tuna Club. The Tuna Club was the first saltwater fishing club in the world, established in 1898 by Charles Frederick Holder who also was involved in the organization of the Rose Parade. The first Tuna Club meetings were held in the old Metropole Hotel until a location was leased on the waterfront and a clubhouse built. The first clubhouse burned in 1915 and soon afterwards the present clubhouse was built with the help of an assessment of the members. Until the 1950's, when the IGFA (International Game Fish Association) assumed the responsibility, the Avalon Tuna Club was the only governing body of saltwater sportfishing in the world. George S. Patton, Cecil B. De Mille, Louie B. Mayer, Keith Spalding and Zane Grey were just a few of the more well known members of the club. Winston Churchill was an honorary member and caught his first billfish on the waters off Catalina Island. When you walk by the club the history jumps out at you. Any Tuna Club member can keep one fascinated for hours with the tales of that establishment. Avalon has something for everyone.

The Coves

Two Harbors is located towards the West end of the island where Isthmus Cove and Catalina (Cat) Harbor almost connect from opposite sides of the island. Two Harbors is a relaxing, laid-back village with a south sea atmosphere complete with palm trees. A lot of movie companies have used this area for a location. Such films as the original "Mutiny on the Bounty" and television shows such as "McHale's Navy" have been filmed here. One could often see such yachts as director John Ford's "Araner" or John Wayne's "Wild Goose" anchored in the deep blue waters of Two Harbors. Isthmus Cove has only a few buildings and is much more remote than Avalon. Camping and hiking enthusiasts seem to frequent this end of the island. The "Reef" (formerly known as "Doug's Harbor Reef") is the one restaurant, but don't let that fool ya, the food is great! There is also a daytime snack bar and at night one can have a Buffalo Milk, ("Milkshake with a KICK!") while being entertained with the sights of the "Star Wars Bar." This nickname is due to the variety of characters you can observe in the bar. Sailors in foulweather gear, beach goers in shorts and tank tops, yachtsmen dressed up, movie stars, fishermen and even a cowboy or two that have been on the island riding horses, can all be in the place at one time, although the horse parking is limited!

One of the many things unique to the cove is their "mall". Yes, the Isthmus enclosed mall. They have everything you need, market, liquor store, mens wear, boutique, hardware store, stationery store, souvenir shop, tackle store, plumbing supply, drug store and even an outboard sales and repair shop, all under one roof. Of course the roof covers only about eighteen hundred square feet. This is one of the most condensed stores anywhere and they usually have what you need! Two Harbors is the gateway to the west. . . well, the west end of the island. If you're looking for open spaces and a place to kick back only a few miles from the coast of southern California, this is that place.

This summer was no different than any other, great weather, fun fishing and great parties at various coves around the island. One place in particular is Fourth of July Cove that has a group of people that do it all. Everyone, no matter what they do for a living, takes turns doing all the jobs and pitching in on all the chores. From Memorial

Day to Labor Day it seems that every weekend they have some sort of organized event. Another great part of their program is the fact all the kids are welcome and have there own area.

Striper Tournaments

In '93 a friend and I decided to enter three marlin tournaments in Catalina. The first one, a local tournament for charity, is the "Church Mouse" as in "poor as a church mouse." Our team had a great time, fished two days with only a couple zips and one early morning confrontation with a sleeper. The team consisted of Chris Kozaites, Tracy Merrill, Alan Schlange and myself fishing on Chris's gameboat "Blues Bros."

The first day we were trolling in calm overcast conditions off of the Avalon bank when Chris spotted a few birds a mile or so away. We changed course, when just below the birds, Alan spotted a marlin sleeping on the surface. Alan went to the bow with Tracy and both prepared to cast live ones on this fish. We slowly slid up to him. Alan cast first, Tracy second. They waited to see if this bad boy was going to take one of the mackerel that were headed towards the safety of the bottom of the boat. At the same time the fish lit up and headed for the area the baits were located. The baits had gone down and the marlin looked as though it was in pursuit as it went down near the bow of the boat. We thought we might have a shot coming up.

At almost the same time another darker object slid next to the marlin. We could not identify it, but it was big. In a few seconds Alan, who had headed back to the stern, following the bait, had a tremendous strike and the reel started to peel. Within a minute Alan had his hands full. Tracy pulled in his bait. The fish was sounding but soon stopped and just hung in there. A couple of minutes later Alan was gaining on the fish when he said he needed to hand off the rod due to a back problem, so Tracy took the rig making the fish an illegal trophy catch. In asking Alan what was wrong, he looked up and said he didn't want to reel the SHARK back in and that was his "back" problem. This was funny and we got a good laugh except of course Tracy, who was on the rod, looking like he had been had! Yeah, in more ways than one. Tracy was reelin' the rig in and as the shark neared the boat he tightened his drag. As Alan went to try to cut the leader the shark jerked and would have pulled Tracy over the side but Alan grabbed him by the waist. You might of thought that Tracy would have let go of the rig. He must be a true fisherman. I'm sure that Tracy would have been a nice snack for that hammerhead, who was not in a great mood at the time. Our team did not place in this tournament, but we finished with the same number of crew we started with!

The next month was September, tournament month in Catalina. First we fished the Catalina Gold Cup, that started off slowly. We had a couple zips the first day and had absolutely no luck with the drop-backs on those zips. The next day, an hour and a half before "stop fishing," we were on top of a school of tuna that a large feeder had been working. We dropped in two live baits and started to slow troll the area. About ten minutes into the trolling there was an explosion on the left rigger. This marlin just knocked the daylights out of the bait and took off. It was a nice fish and might very well be a contender. I was the angler on this fish and we had him close in about fifteen minutes. The marlin came up behind the boat and was moving slow since he was tailwrapped. We stopped the boat and I wound him towards the boat, his tail to us. He suddenly became unwrapped, turned and headed for the boat, as he did so he lit up again. He was closing in on the transom as I reeled like a madman. The leader appeared and the wireman grabbed it. The fish was lit up like a Las Vegas Casino and would be a tough gaff. The gaffman was ready and as the wireman pulled the marlin to the boat the thrashing fish spit the hook. A moment of silence that seems to last forever, whenever a fish gets unbuttoned. Oh well, that's why it's called fishing and not catching!

The last tournament the team would do this year in Catalina was the inaugural Catalina Classic, the end of September. We arrived at the island the day before and went in to Avalon for the sign up and evening's festivities. I had fished the whole week before on my own boat and had a good idea where the fish might be. With the computer hooked up to the phone, on "Blues Bros," we had a constant up-date on the water temperature breaks in the area from Ocean Imaging. That always seemed to be the areas holding the fish.

The next morning "Blues Bros" was lined up for the shotgun start and off we went. Visibility was not good as we took off and it became foggy with zero-zero visibility

"Blues Bros" Team: Mike, Alan, Tracy & Capt. Chris

soon after the start of the tournament. So there we were, doing twenty knots and couldn't see our hand in front of our face, hoping the radar didn't give out. About thirty minutes later we slowed to trolling speed and got the gear wet. As soon as we were able to see that the lure pattern was right, the generator decided to shut down, so far this day was not going so well. Chris and I jumped down in the engine room to see what could be done to get THIS problem solved. We were in the bilge for a few minutes when all of a sudden the main engines slowed down to idle and were shifted into neutral. Both Chris and I looked at each other and wondered what we did to cause that! Meanwhile Tracy was yelling at us to get our butts on deck. In the fog we came up on a pack of sleepers, Alan ran to the bow, cast a live bait and was immediately "bit." The gear aft was cleared and the fight was on. This was a nice marlin and he made Alan work for it. The fish took off, jumped a few times and then took off again. We backed down and were able to get this fish wired in about twenty minutes. Since it was the first fish of the tournament we put the fish aboard and slipped him into a cold insulated fish bag to help preserve him until we could get him weighed in. Later that day we weighed him in at Rosie's fish market on the pier in Avalon. We found ourselves leading the tournament with a 155-pound striped marlin. A bit of celebrating that night but we still had our work cut out for us the next day. We were leading the tournament until late the following day when over the radio we heard of a couple fish being taken near Church Rock, at the east end of Catalina Island. We had one shot early in the morning on a single sleeper but he did not have the competitive drive that seems to occur when there is more than one sleeper, we didn't get bit. As the time came to a close we were in third place and the two fish that bumped us back were both over two hundred pounds, not bad for Catalina. It's always nice to place in any tournament.

Chapter 5

Vernski/The Chief

There have been many good things said about the people of the Carolinas and I have to hand it to them, they are friendly and they make some great boats. A few years ago Scotty Lewis "Vernski" flew to South Carolina to deliver a new 65-foot Hatteras sportfisher to California with Joe Mike Lopez as the Captain. The preparation for the trip to Newport Beach, California, via the Panama Canal, lasted for about two and a half weeks. One evening early into the project they were out having dinner when after a short conversation with the restaurant owner Vern found out that they were cousins! Howdy Cuz! From then on Vern was cuz Vern-Bob, Joe Mike was Joe Mike-Bob and all the dinners and drinks were on the house until they departed.

Cabo San Lucas

A couple years before the trip to the Amazon River on "Horizons", Mitch, myself and Vern had delivered the 46-foot Merritt sportfisher "French Look" to San Diego, California, from Cabo San Lucas, in September, for a refit. Well known Australian gameboat Captain,

French Look I in San Diego departing for Cabo

Laurie Wright, who normally skippered the "French Look," had departed for Australia from Cabo via Los Angeles to fish the season on the "reef." He had asked Mitch to take over for the trip north and while the boat would be in refit in San Diego.

September is the height of hurricane season in Mexico and its a little erie to be in Cabo when there are not many other boats there. As soon as we departed, the seas and southerly winds from a hurricane a couple hundred miles south of Cabo gave us a good push for the first two hundred miles

French Look I, Tyson's Pride side tied to Horizons in Magdalena Bay

north. The trip took only three days with almost no wind except for the southerly near Cabo, nice and boring (boring is good). After we arrived in San Diego Vernski flew down to Australia to work as one of the fishing deckhands for Laurie.

After the refit in late October Mitch, myself, and a fishing mate from the East Coast delivered "French Look" back to Cabo. We had a short stop in Magdalena Bay to side tie with the Tyson boats, "Horizons" and "Tyson's Pride," for a Mexican dinner on the "Horizons" before heading for Cabo that night. It was quite a sight to see two Merritt boats side tied to "Horizons." Little did Mitch know that in a couple years he would take over as the Captain on "Horizons."

The day after our arrival in Cabo, the owner of "French Look" Jean Paul Richard, arrived and we fished a week straight. We used the "bait and switch" method. Trolling four hookless teasers and religiously watching the teasers for any fins in the wake. At

the same time there were four rigs set up, ready to drop back at any given time. Eight, twelve, sixteen and twenty-pound test rigs were set up with an imported Florida ballyhoo rigged to each one. The baits were set on aluminum foil on top of the ice in the chest behind the rocket launcher. That was in place of the normal fighting chair.

On the first day a couple of striped marlin came into the teasers, we successfully released one of them. The next day we were outside the Jamie Bank and a group of four stripers came up behind the teasers at the same time. We teased the marlin closer to the back of the boat while Jean Paul dropped a twelve-pound rig back. As the ballyhoo slipped back near the area of the stripers, a blue marlin came in and sucked down the bait. The seas were flat and the blue marlin dug in. This marlin went off, greyhounding for the South Seas. After his first run the fish sounded, then stalled. Mitch spun "French Look" around the fish, which was straight below us. Jean Paul was able to get a bit of line back. The marlin seemed to be confused by the boat spinning above him, causing the line to pull in different directions.

Jean Paul Richard, French Look I;
250 LB Blue Marlin, 12 LB test off Cabo San Lucas.

Jean Paul is an experienced light line angler and it was quite a show watching him handle this fish. We were on the fish for four and a half hours of back downs, spins and nice angling by Jean Paul. The fish was wired just before dark and released. Bait and switch is a lot of fun, and obviously the longer any team fishes together the better the results.

Cabo night life can be pretty crazy, the beaches are beautiful, but the best thing I've found about Cabo since first coming here in 1969 is that this is one of the most consistent fishing areas in the world year round. The blue marlin season is not necessarily all year but you never know. A few years ago in February, normally not a good time of the year for blue marlin, we were trolling up to Los Frailes anchorage. After a mediocre day on the Gordo Bank a three hundred-pound plus blue marlin hit the right short corner. The mahi, tuna, wahoo and rooster fish are around Cabo on and off all year. It still amazes me how much fish Cabo produces considering how many boats fish the area daily.

Panama

We fished "French Look" in Cabo for a week before I had to leave for California. A couple weeks later Laurie and Vern came back from the reef. With Mitch the three of them moved the boat to Panama. If you have not been to the Tropic Star Lodge in Pinas Bay, make the trip! Mike, Terri and Zane Andrews are the perfect hosts in paradise. They have twelve identical Bertram 31 gameboats in excellent shape. Each is a different color and each is named for a different country of the world. All are powered with the same 453 G.M. diesels. Mike showed us through the maintenance shop were we observed why the boats are in great shape. They even have a spare engine ready to go if needed! A beautifully groomed and well maintained resort make it a pleasant stay ashore when the fishing is over for the day. There have been over one hundred and forty five world records broken here. Being only a few hours from Miami, the lodge is booked almost all season, so get your reservations in early. Vern said the fishing in Pinas Bay, Panama was some of the best he'd ever experienced.

They released a lot of very large marlin, both Pacific blue and black marlin, breaking the eight-pound line world record with a 462-pound black marlin. They did not have any "shots" (strikes) on any fish that would have been near the all tackle record for either species.

Comets Please!

I first met "Vern" in the mid eighties in Newport Beach, California, when he was working on a sportfisher named "Bottom Line." Vern was looking for another job that would be fishing more and landed the deckhand job on "Rumline," a 54-foot Striker that had been purchased by a friend of mine, Pat Farrah. "Rumline" was the new name and had just been changed after the boat was brought around from Cozumel, Mexico, via the Panama Canal. The boat was well known back east from its previous name, "Poverty Sucks." A few had tried to persuade Pat into keeping that name, but he didn't think it was good for P.R. and business. This was also when I first met Mitch. He was hired to run the boat, so he flew in from Australia and soon found how cold California could be in the winter. "Rumline" fished California waters for the summer then headed for Mexico in early November. So.... Vern and Mitch, what a pair.

This was the year that Haley's Comet was in the vicinity and would not be visible again for another eighty years. I managed to make it to Cabo San Lucas for a few fishing trips. On one trip I was able to have my wife Linda, her parents, and my parents all go down for a few days on "Rumline." In the evenings we anchored at Los Frailes about forty miles north of Cabo up in the gulf. This was a great spot to view the comet because there was no town, only a couple of homes, so the night sky was dark and crystal clear. It was so clear that the comet could be seen beautifully with just the naked eye and with the binoculars the tail was easily visible. The whole group stayed up late into the night to observe the comet. The fishing sucked so we slept in most mornings.

King Ka-Chammy-Chammy (chamois)

Vern was talented at a number of things, fishing, cooking and cleaning. He has been a fishing mate since HE was a little bait and he knows his stuff in the cockpit. Vern, whose real name is Scotty Lewis, is known back east as the "The Chief." No matter where he is or which name he is known by he is one of the top mates in the world in any condition, on any boat and with any size fish. The guy is also a master on the barbecue and Vern's wahoo steaks are locally world famous. But, his job after fishing was cleaning and detailing the boat. Vern being the hard-headed son of a gun he is, would always insist on doing the wash down himself. I suppose this was so he could grumble about it. Once I started to help him and he almost bit my friggin' head off. Thus he was King at chamoising off the boat. We gave him the title "King Ka-Chammmy-Chammy (chamois)."

Aloha

After the trip to Mexico, Pat decided to take "Rumline" to Hawaii. Mitch, Vern, Jeff Beal and myself were the crew for this job. The preparation was all up to Mitch and Vern. They added extended, deeper, rudder caps for better steerage in big following seas, portable fuel tanks, since there are not too many fuel stations between California and Hawaii (none). Small injectors were installed for better fuel consumption, storm windows to keep the seas from breaking into the salon in case we get into big seas, etc. It took quite a while to get ready. Mitch calculated we could cross the 2,225 miles using only one gallon per mile between both engines and the generator. That got a good laugh from a lot of people. The crossing from the Los Angeles area to Hawaii is the longest span of open water in the world without an alternate port of refuge. At one point during our preparation, an acquaintance of Pat's tried to get us to sign a waiver for liability. This in case we perished along the way, what a bone-head idea that was. Needless to say when Pat found out about this he was furious, there was no waiver.

Pat and Mitch arranged for a sixty-foot schooner to go with us for the first six hundred miles to refuel us at that point with nine hundred gallons of diesel. This was Pat's wish and, although Mitch did not think it was necessary, it made for a nice reserve. As a matter of fact we arrived in Hilo, Hawaii, with fourteen hundred gallons of fuel aboard, averaging only one point one gallons of diesel fuel per mile.

The trip took eleven days and it ended up being one of the best fishing trips of our lives, we caught fish every day! The first day we caught a couple of albacore tuna. The next few days we caught yellowfin tuna and eventually started to catch mahi-mahi and more tuna, as the water temperature started to warm up.

In the middle of the trip we released a 160-pound striped marlin. With ten to twelve-foot following seas it didn't take long to figure out that backing down was NOT a good idea, especially with over twice the designed fuel load on board. Using a Penn 130 rig we just idled down swell as Jeff reeled the little marlin in for a quick release.

At one point towards the end of the trip, we were throwing overboard the frozen dinners we had, to make room for the fish. Vern boated a fifty-pound wahoo (ono) as we neared the harbor at Kona, the day after our first landfall in Hilo. It looked like a fire drill as the barefoot crew scattered out of the cockpit as Vern tossed the fish on to the deck. The teeth on these fish are razor sharp and it always seems that wahoo try to "flop" your way when they are first boated.

Pat had a lot of fun using his boat in Hawaii and Vern was able to chamois to his heart's content. One evening Vern was entertaining a friend on "Rumline" when Pat unexpectedly showed up from the mainland. Vern about died. Pat walked in and, being a master of reading people and situations, he immediately apologized to Vern (his deck hand) for walking in on him and his lady friend. Pat, taking the role of the deck hand asked, "Sir, may I pour you a drink or get you anything else?" Typical Vern, seeing what Pat was up to, ordered up a couple of drinks that Pat made for them. After making the cocktails he asked Vern if there was anything else he could do for them before he left. After Vern asked him to turn the stereo down, Pat departed. To say the least Vern is still indebted to Pat for that one!

Lahaina

In the eighties "Rumline" did a lot of tournaments. One day Pat called to see if I would like to do the Lahaina Jackpot Tournament. I flew over the next day and had a ball, in fact we placed second in the mahi division and won an eighty-wide Penn International with a fish I caught on the second day of the tournament. The one particular point about the Lahaina tournament is that they encourage lots of participation. They do this with small entry fees and lots of prizes, with the help of a lot of sponsorship. That can be attributed to a lot of time and hard work by the Lahaina Yacht Club members. The majority of the one hundred and thirty-five entries are what some call mosquito boats, basically a class of boats that are trailerable with single diesels, which are fast, economical and portable. The state of Hawaii has a minimum number of slips because legislators feel that more marinas would ruin more reef areas. The trophies are great, an entry can only win one trophy. There are divisions for mahi, ono, marlin and tuna, with places first through fifth for each division. So if a boat weighs in the largest marlin it cannot win any other prize no matter what else they have caught. They also encourage releasing small marlin. The largest marlin caught as of this year's tournament was around seven hundred pounds. The bottom line is that this is a fun tournament for everyone.

The Sin Twisters

Pat and I were the only anglers on "Rumline" in this Lahaina tournament. A fisherman from Homer, Alaska, asked if he could fish with us, even offered to pay his own entry, which Pat declined. We now had three anglers. The tournament has a Shot Gun start, where all the boats line up, waiting for the signal before they can take off full speed for the area that they each think is going to produce the winning fish. So off we went the first day for the north shore of Molokai Island. It was a typical day with huge ground swells, twenty knots of wind and lots of chop. This was not exactly what Pat wanted since he is prone to getting a little seasick. Matter of fact, the guy from Alaska was the same. We spent the whole day on the backside of Molokai without much luck.

The next day I found myself as the only angler, both Pat and our guest did not appear for the day's fishing. "Rumline" headed for the north shore of Maui this time and in the middle of the afternoon, caught our second place mahi-mahi. When that fish struck, he hit hard enough to make anyone not watching think it was a marlin. The next and also last day we didn't have a zip.

If you have never been in Lahaina on Halloween it is just like Mardi Gras. Front Street is closed, everyone dresses up and the place goes wild. That night was Halloween and was it a party! We had the boat at the fuel dock for the night and a guard. That's the night the Alaskan met the sin twisters, or is that the twin sisters? He brought these two girls to the boat, they were exact twins, and hammered out of their minds. In the slurring of their own words they came up with the change from twin sisters to sin twisters. Anyway there was a small crowd on and around the boat. All met the illustrious sin twisters, er.... twin sisters. One twin's boyfriend finally took them home, after the rum was almost gone. I wonder how he could tell them apart?

The next day we had another get-together and Mitch had the task of entertaining his

2nd place Mahi, worth a penn 80 wide, 1986 Jackpot
Rumline Team: Capt. Mitch, Mike, Jackpot Queen;
kneeling - Trevor, Scott Lewis, AKA Chief/Vernski; absent- owner Pat Farrah

girlfriend(s). One from Honolulu, one from Lahaina, and one from Kona, and none of them knew of the other before this. The girls from Honolulu and Kona separately had decided to surprise him by showing up in Lahaina and boy was he surprised! He had one girl in the tuna tower, one in the bridge and one in the salon. He actually kept this going for almost an hour before one of the young ladies became a bit upset and realizing what was up, she departed. The other two soon caught on but each wanted the other to leave. I'm not sure what happened after that, the rum and afternoon sun were kicking in, but I do believe that he ended up taking both of them out to dinner. That-a-way Mitchy boy.

Party's Over

After one tournament in Kona found the double hooks too close, disqualifying a first place fish, then losing an engine during another Kona tournament, Pat did not take much time in responding to a local yacht broker's offer. A wealthy Japanese man offered twice what he paid for the boat, before commissions. When the job goes away, so does the crew, so Mitch flew to Australia to run a boat on the reef and Vern had a mate job waiting for him in Florida.

Chapter 6

HELLO! Back To the Present

uh... Ah... Well... it was a fun summer in Catalina. The tournaments and trips to the different coves at the island are fun but as it does every year, the weather changes and it starts to get cold. In fact everyone starts getting colds! Al Bento phoned, "Lahaina tournament this October?" My response, "Of course! Yeah! Sure! Love to! See ya in late October!" Late in October I was off to Honolulu to meet Al and help take the "Alele II" to Maui.

Lahaina '93, A World Tournament Record

Al,.. Al Bento, what can you say about this ol' Portugue? Lots! He was born in Hawaii of Portuguese decent. Al has done almost everyone I know. No, wait!... Let me get this right, Al has done almost everyone I know A FAVOR at one time or another. "Ask Al, he'll help out." Al takes the kids fishing, pulls sailboats off the rocks during the Friday night races in front of Hawaii Yacht Club, cleans the kids' fish and has even been known to take the ladies out on the Wahine Tournaments. Ladies always make Al smile! Al is the owner of a Radon 35 named "Alele II" and makes a living fishing, with rod and reel. Al is also a representative of IGFA (International Game Fish Association) in Hawaii and a past Commodore of Hawaii Yacht Club.

One thing about going to Hawaii is that you can fly over to Hawaii after a long day at work in California and still be there by 11:00 p.m. which is when I arrived. Al met me at the airport and off we went to his home for a couple of hours of sleep before we shoved off for Maui in the morning. When we arrived at the house, Rhonda was still up so we had a quick beer and did a little yaking before hitting the sack.

Five a.m. comes early when you've been flying anywhere! We were up early and off to "Alele II" down at Hawaii Yacht Club. Boy we've had some times in that place. In fact, if I try, I might be able to remember a few. When we arrived we found Frenchy had arrived before us. Yeah, he passed out a couple hours ago, and was sprawled out on the starboard engine cover. You could smell his breath from the parking lot. We were careful not to wake him until absolutely necessary. If we were to wake him, he might light up a smoke and blow his friggin' head off, (from his own fumes). Al and I pulled out the five 130 Penn International rigs out of the cabin and started rigging the boat for the trip to Molokai and later to Lahaina, Maui. After half an hour we were ready to go. After Al had checked the port engine levels we moved Frenchy from the starboard engine box to the port engine box so Al could check the starboard engine levels, Frenchy was paralyzed.

The dawn was well on its way when we departed the entrance to Alawai Harbor. It is always a good idea to get across the Molokai Channel early in the day when the trade winds were more likely to be down. This trip was not too bad, wind at fifteen knots and the seas at ten feet, the usual. After a couple cups of luke warm coffee, a soggy sweet roll, and a bit of salt spray we were in the lee of Molokai Island. The lines had been out since we departed and so far nothing. We headed for the "CC" fishing buoy on the way to the island of Lanai. The State of Hawaii has set yellow fishing buoys (FADs) around the islands to attract fish. We trolled towards the "CC" buoy and spotted a large flock of birds going ape over something in the water below. Half a mile from the bird pile the center rigger popped and seconds later the rig below started singing. I grabbed the pole and took my time winding in a nice fifty-pound ahi (yellow fin tuna). As we continued trolling, both riggers that were wound in close to the boat while we were fighting the ahi popped. We found ourselves with a double ahi bite! A short ten minutes later we boated a couple more nice ahi. Watching Frenchy's face as he had to lean over the rail to gaff those ahi was hilarious. He still hadn't recovered from the previous evening. We trolled the area for a while and after collecting a few more ahi, headed off for the island of Lanai. Lunch was Al's poki (raw fish, marinated with onions and spices), smoked marlin and a couple of Budweisers. A few miles off the Lanai coast we had a couple zips from a curious marlin but neither of these stuck. Almost immediately we hooked up with two nice mahi-mahi. The two mahi tried to wrap us up but eventually they made their way into the fishbox. These two weighed around forty pounds each.

Lahaina Harbor is not very big but Al had managed to arrange for a slip next to one of the more successful charter boats in Lahaina, the "Hinatea," with Captain Mark Schultz. After we fueled we were secure in the slip by five-thirty. Another boat, gear and crew wash down, then off to Lahaina Yacht Club for dinner and to see what else might be cookin'.

Lahaina Yacht Club ribs are as good as the ones served on cafe "Desperado," Scott Guenther's 57-foot sportfisher. Whether in Mexico or California, he serves the best ribs in the west! Anyway Lahaina Yacht Club's are as close as you can get and quantity is not a problem either!

Frenchy and I were almost finished eating by the time Al finished saying "Hi" to all of his friends. As Al finally ate dinner we had another Cuba Libre and let them ribs settle. Al said the scuttlebutt was the same, both the fishing and the beer were cold. Oh well, the tournament was still a few days away. After solving all the world's problems we bunked down on "Alele II."

Ribs on Cafe "Desperado"

The next morning we awoke to find Kitty sitting on the covering board having a cold Bud, quiet as ever. Kitty looks at Al and says "Unca Al, How you ben' brudda?" Al looks up with the one open eye and says "Hey Kitty, how ya ben' doin?" With that Al extends his hand and they shake.

Kitty is Hawaiian and has lived his whole life in Maui. Diving for black coral is what he does and is also why he has a large scar on his stomach. He came up too fast one time, his stomach ruptured and he lived! Al and Kitty have been friends a long time. Kitty always looks out for Al when he's in Lahaina, just as long as the cooler's full. We must have talked with Kitty and his friends for a few hours about diving, fishing etc., all the stuff that had been going on for the last year or so.

Kitty was talking about a big blue marlin that they had on two weeks before and said "Da fish jumped and greyhounded across da Pacific a long ways...bing...bing...bing," motioning with his hands like a marlin jumping.

The one thing everyone mentioned was the fact the fishing had been off and that no big fish had been taken for a while, but it was still two days before the start of the tournament.

After a nutritious breakfast at the local "B.K. Lounge" (Burger King) we started going over all the gear on board. Re-rigging all the lures, new doubles on all the rigs, engine checks, spares checks, on and on until it started to get dark. An early night by our standards and even a couple of hours of real sleep felt good. We awoke around seven the next morning. It would be another day of getting the boat and gear checked and double checked before we headed for the Do Jo (doe-joe) Mission where the tournament pre-dinner and meeting were to be held that evening. Later in the morning Phil, one more of our tournament team members, showed up to give us a hand. Phil runs the sugar cane factory in Lahaina and told us that due to last year's tournament he had quit drinking, I suppose that meant there was hope for us!

That evening we all drove down to the mission for the meeting and once again Al surfaced from the crowd for dinner just as they were about to quit serving. He has a lot of friends. After dinner the officials had a briefing on the procedures for the next three days and as soon as they finished the country western band kicked in, Hawaiian style. Not to let the ladies down, our crew spun a few of em' around the dance floor before retiring to the boat for a good night's sleep.

The boats were all lined up for the 7:00 a.m. Shot Gun start. The signal was given and we were off, heading for the buoy off the north shore of Molokai Island. As far as you could see boats were heading in every direction with no one particular area being focused on by any, the spread was pretty even. We ran for about ten miles and dropped em' in the water about five miles into the channel between Maui and Molokai. The wind was at twelve knots and seas were seven feet, not bad for the channel. We had it pretty quiet until we neared the buoy at the top of the channel where there were five boats, two soaking baits and the others trolling the area.

We were trolling five lines at the time, when Al asked me to throw out a feather lure to catch a small tuna. The feather was only in the water for a few minutes when we hooked up. As soon as we boated the ten-pound (Aku) tuna, Al rigged it for trolling and immediately set up one of the heavy rigs for "the-tuna-slow-troll." Within a few minutes we were in the vicinity of the buoy and had pulled in the other lines. On our second circle around the buoy the rubber band on the left rigger snapped, we were bit. The fish slapped the tuna and took off. We were certain that we'd have a shot at a good fish out here. A few brief moments later the reel was peeling line out and as soon as it started, it stopped, even before one of us could pull it out of the covering board and put it in the chair. What had hit the tuna had all but cut it in half and it wasn't a shark, no teeth marks.

We started trolling again, spending more time in the area where we were bit but all we could raise were a couple small Aku tunas on the feather, which we used to slow troll to no avail. Off we went, to the buoy down the Island of Molokai towards the Kalaupapa Peninsula light house at the old Leper Colony. As the afternoon went by we tried everything. As the end of the day's fishing came closer we trolled towards Lahaina, day one and nada. At least we had a couple of days left in the tournament.

Things had gone differently over on "Cormorant," a beautiful 54-foot Buddy Davis owned by Bruce Matson. At today's start he had gone the other way, towards the Alenuihaha Channel that separates the islands of Maui and Hawaii. On this particular day there was no wind there but the seas were still up, with ocean swells up to ten feet. One crew member, "Haole boy," said they had a problem getting any of the lures to swim right and ended up trolling the largest lures they had just to get them to swim effectively.

They were working the "JJ" buoy area off the southern end of Kahoolawe Island when late in the afternoon this marlin came into the wake, gobbled the left short corner lure and didn't even know she was hooked. The fish then proceeded to take a hit at the right corner, then headed to the right rigger, then over to the left rigger, and eventually back to the left corner, where she was first hooked. The fish then took off and the fight was on. Everyone aboard "Cormorant" knew they had a big marlin, but I don't think any of them really knew how big this fish was. The local crew on board had a lot of big fish experience and if anyone could land this fish they could.

An hour later the fish was nearing the boat, she could have been gaffed, except she was still lit-up. The gaff man looked at the fish, then at the wire man and said "I'm not going to gaff that fish, he's too green." The wire man looked at the gaff man and said, "I'm not going to wire the fish if your not going to gaff the fish, especially if he's way too green." Then they both looked at the angler as the fish made another run.

The problem was after that last death run the fish died. When a large fish dies it is necessary to plane the fish up with the boat and angler working together. At first, they lined up the boat into the swells and went ahead very slowly, then stopped and backed down very quickly to allow the angler to reel up a little bit of line. This process went on for ever, letting the angler get more line each time. Well, it worked for "Cormorant." Each time they were able to get the fish closer and eventually were able to gaff the beast.

The next problem was to get the fish on board, or as much as possible on board. If you have a block and tackle, you hook it up and pull the marlin in head first through the transom door. With everyone pushing, pulling and even trying to "float" the fish in the door, it can be a bear of a job to boat a fish this big. They did all of the above plus some. The fact the fish was in excess of sixteen feet meant he'd be having lunch in the galley if they ever got him all the way in the boat, across the cockpit and through the salon door. The fish was in the boat except for the last seven feet. They lassoed the tail and hauled ass towards the harbor at Lahaina. From hook up to boating the fish it took three and a half hours.

As the "Alele II" headed back to Lahaina near the end of Maui we heard one boat relay a call from "Cormorant" to tournament control. The message was that they had just boated their fish and were on their way in. Due to the small size of Lahaina Harbor and the weigh-in facility, a line forms just outside the harbor entrance and it's first come first serve. This evening there were at least fifteen boats waiting to weigh in their fish. Another message that was barely audible over the CB channel said "Cormorant" was also transmitting channel 71 on the VHF radio. The officials operated the tournament over CB radio per request of the Coast Guard. We set our VHF on channel 71 and overheard Bruce talking with the officials of the tournament. He was asking for permission to come in and weigh his fish as soon as he arrived at the harbor. The officials asked if they had an emergency. Bruce stated that they had a fish that was partially in the salon, over the whole cockpit deck and the last third of the fish was hanging out through the transom door in the wake of the boat. They were worried that when they slowed down that the fish might be subject to being attacked by sharks. One Hawaiian fisherman on the VHF radio, cut in saying in local slang, "De need no Tiger (shark) in da tank, Bra!" The officials asked for Cormorant's ETA. "Cormorant" replied they would be in the area in thirty minutes. The officials said they would advise them in a couple minutes and for "Cormorant" to stand-by on both the CB and VHF. A few seconds later the tournament officials asked over the CB radio if any of the boats in line would mind if "Cormorant" weighed in their fish upon arrival, the reason being the fish was hanging out the back by six or seven feet. Everyone agreed to let them come in out of order. One Hawaiian guy said, "If da fish is dat big, let him come in just so da rest of us can see it, brah."

When "Cormorant" arrived we had just pulled into our slip, I headed down to watch the weigh-in. As "Cormorant" backed into the weigh-in area at the fuel dock the fish looked awesome. It actually hung out the back at least seven feet, this is a Buddy Davis 54-foot sportfisher! The weigh-in crew used a pole lift to get the tail up and almost pulled the lift out of the wall it was cemented into. The fish was all the way to the top of the pole lift and still had its bill in the water. The crew had to pull the fish by hand to get it on the dock. The next task was to put the fish on two carts and wheel it over to the weigh-in area. The number of people needed to put the fish on the carts and hold it in place while being rolled to the weigh-in area was something else, ten people. The IGFA certified scale was strong enough to hold the fish, but was the electric lift or, for that matter, was the pole holding the electric lift, going to be strong enough? The biggest fish ever caught in this tournament in the past was in the seven hundred-pound range, by the "Cutty Sark." The fish was wheeled under the lift and after a bit of a hassle the officials started to lift the fish. Everything was okay until the line around the tail started to cut into the tail. The lift was reversed and the fish quickly laid back down. The tail was re-tied a couple inches lower and more wraps were used. The second lift was going well until the last four feet when the electric motor started to smoke and make all kinds of noise. The officials stopped the motor for a rest and gave it a try a couple minutes later. This time the lift pulled the fish all the way up. The IGFA electronic scale took off and stopped at 1,199.5 pounds. The crowd went crazy. Champagne was spraying everywhere. The crew onboard "Cormorant" were exuberant. A few days after the tournament the scale was re-certified and was found to be a pound and a half light so the weight of this fish was updated to 1,201 pounds even. Quite a fish!

Cormorant's fish – 1,201 lbs

When I went back to the boat, Al, Kitty, Phil, and Frenchy were all having a cold Bud when I mentioned how much the fish weighed. Frenchy said "Holy shit," Phil just smiled and shook his head, Kitty went off, "What a fight dat must a ben, bing... bing... bing," with his hands in the air as though he was holding a rod. Al just said, "Well, not only is that the largest fish in this tournament, it's the largest fish in any tournament in the world, looks like we're fishing for second place!"

Kitty was fishing on a mosquito boat that is a lot smaller than Al's boat, but trailerable and very fast. In the past the mosquito boats have done very well in this tournament, even winning it a few times. There are a couple of manufacturers building these boats in Hawaii. They are fiberglass with a lot of flare in the bow and usually have a single diesel. Kitty said, "If we'd caught dat fish, we'd a probably either sunk or da marlin would of been hit by da sharks if we'd a side-tied dim and brought dim in bing... bing... bing." We all had another cold Bud.

You know it is a funny feeling you get when a competitor does well, especially if you have been on their team in the past or have helped them out in some way. One feeling of congratulation and another feeling of being unhappy that it wasn't yourself winning, good ol' human nature. "Congratulations, I want to kick you butt" is the best way I can put the feeling that a lot of people had after that fish was weighed in. The fact is Bruce Matson and his crew on "Cormorant" kicked everyone's ass with that fish, not only did it win, it is the largest fish caught in any tournament in the world! Nice job!

That evening we did something different, we went to Lahaina Yacht Club and had the ribs! A lot of stories passed across the bar that night about the time everyone had lost the big one at one time or another. When the crew from "Cormorant" arrived there was a big applause, lots of cocktails and backslapping for the boys.

The next day we took off from the line and headed for the Alenuihaha Channel via the channel between Maui and Kahoolawe Island. As we went by Molokini Island, which is primarily a diving island used by a lot of different charter vessels, we caught a nice mahi-mahi, weighing around thirty-five pounds. This fish would be out of the prize category by at least ten pounds.

As we neared the rugged cliffs at the northern end of Kahoolawe the wind and seas picked up considerably, wind twenty knots, seas twelve feet and we were abeam to these conditions. The Alenuihaha Channel would be very ugly today. We were only a couple of miles from the coast of Kahoolawe Island with the sheer cliffs on our lee side. At this point it would be difficult to fight a fish, while the seas were abeam. The idea was to make the "I" buoy near the end of Kahoolawe Island and then run down swell towards the "JJ" buoy, off the southeast corner of the island.

I was sitting up on the starboard side of the bridge with my foul weather jacket on, facing aft and watching the lures, while Al was driving and just trying to see through all the water flying up on the bridge. All this while we were trying to quarter the seas a bit. Phil and Frenchy were in the cockpit, just hanging on. A couple minutes earlier we had run through a school of porpoise that were fading off in the wake. Meanwhile, I noticed a dark object trailing the left short corner lure. At first I thought it might be another porpoise but it didn't come up for air and it was moving in a different way. The sunlight and the super clear water allowed a line of sight so you could see a long way into the water under and behind the lures. After a few of seconds I told Al, "I think we have company." He looked at me with salt water all over his head, face, glasses and says, "What the *@!#* are you talking about?" I said, "I think we're about to get bit on the left short corner," and as I finished saying that, the fish that appeared to be a porpoise a minute ago was now in pursuit of the lure. At first the fish was under the lures and all of it's appendages seemed to be folded up, then as the fish came in for the lure it came up to the surface. Its dorsal and tail fin were aggressively breaking the water and simultaneously it lit up like a Las Vegas casino. This marlin was on a mission! The fish, as large as a porpoise, exploded on the left short corner lure, then took off like a striped-ass ape. Al looks at me, the fish, the location against the island, the seas and says, "Oh, #@*!@! great!" As I went down the ladder I yelled up at Al and jokingly said, "Timing is everything!"

It was Phil's turn to be angler. Between barfs, he took the rod out of the covering board and was almost pulled over the side by the fish, but he managed to get in the chair. The blue marlin was easily in excess of five hundred pounds, which was second place at this point. Al, since he didn't have a lot of down swell running room, put the bow into the

63

seas as the fish headed off for Maui and deeper water. The first run didn't last too long and within twenty minutes Phil had the fish turned and actually was gaining line on it. The marlin was coming towards the right corner of the boat and at one point was only one hundred feet away. The fish had done a slow loop from the left corner, out aft and then back to the right corner area, and did this without doing any radical turns himself. When he was close I noticed the hook as Al pushed the throttles forward a bit so as not to let the fish pass the boat or turn. Al had noticed the same thing, the fish was bill hooked. If we could keep him from turning we might get a gaff shot but it would have to be soon and before he turned. A moment later the fish did a slow turn towards the boat and, as if in slow motion, we watched the hook slide off the bill.

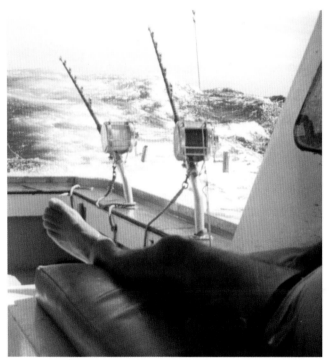

Finally running down swell on "Alele II"

Adios! Time for a cold Bud. I told Al, "Well, when you know your @#!*&#@ (screwed), you're not all bad!" Al just smiled, shook his head and started up to trolling speed while we put the rigs out. Phil did appreciate the fact that within the hour we were running down swell a few miles off of Kahoolawe heading for the buoy at the other end of the island, his color was almost normal. If the fight had gone on much longer the fish may have won.

The afternoon was slipping away as we worked the buoy without any results. When end of fishing time was gettin' close we headed for the barn. It was quite late when we entered the harbor and took our slip. Al's engines had quite a few hours on them so he never ran the boat hard, which would help prevent any engine problems that might keep us from fishing at all. The usual gear, boat and crew wash down and off to dinner. Tonight something different, Kobie Steak House and of course we all ordered RIBS! NO, NO, not really, we all had a great steak dinner! To say the least we sacked in a lot earlier.

On this, the second day, all of the places in the categories of fish had been filled, so, to place, all we had to do is land a bigger fish in any of those categories. This tournament attracted a lot of boats because each boat could only win one prize. With places in all categories first through fifth and largest fish first through tenth, a lot of boats would receive a prize. The money went for the largest fish, first through tenth, and all the rest of the prizes were rods and reels, all Penn Internationals, from 130's to the smallest prize of 50-wide reels. There were also a lot of raffle prizes, the boat names were picked basically out of a box and, again, only one prize per boat. These raffle prizes were also rods and reels.

Day three and the same program, Shot Gun start and off to the buoy off the southern end of Kahoolawe Island. We started trolling five miles from the starting area. A couple of years ago a Hawaiian sampan was only a few miles from the starting area and had a strike on a 130 Penn rig. She was spooled before they could turn the boat around. Sampans are Hawaiian built boats that are usually around fifty feet or so, with a high bow and a deeper "V" shaped bottom in the bows to keep them from pounding. They have a large cabin and are a great sea boat. Their only problem is that they are not real fast and usually start fishing immediately at the starts.

An hour later we had a tremendous strike on the left rigger. It turned out to be another mahi-mahi about twenty-five pounds. As we headed out for the buoy Al spotted a pack of birds and off we went, rigging our small tuna rigs which we set as we neared the birds. It did not take long to catch a nice eight-pound aku and rig it for a slow troll. We were only a mile or so from the buoy so we slow-trolled over that way. After passing the buoy we had started to turn when we had a strike on the right rigger where the tuna was. The reel started letting out, I jumped on the rig and with the reel in free spool I let a few seconds or so go by before deciding to set the hook. As soon as I did the fish went straight down, we figured it was probably a large ahi. The line was going out quickly and after a minute the line went slack. I know we didn't get bit-off or break the line, so I reeled the rig in. The bait was still there but a bit beat-up and it appeared that we had been hit by a large ahi from the markings on the bait.

This did not appear to be our week and as this day ticked away we made our way back to Lahaina. Today we arrived back at the harbor at a decent time of five-thirty. Today was October thirty-first, Halloween. Bus loads of people come in from all over the island and people fly in from as far away as the mainland to be in Lahaina for Halloween.

After a quick clean up, we had reservations at the Aloha Cantina and glad of that. Front Street was a madhouse at seven o'clock. After dinner we watched the parade come down the street and as soon as it was over we walked the street just to see all the outfits. It was definitely a party! Young and old, everyone was having a good time. We thought we might have used a couple of these costumes as lures, during the past week. Since we were not in costume we probably were the ones that stuck out. We ran across Bruce Matson and a couple of the crew and listened to the story of their fish. Maybe, next year Al. His dream, like a lot of saltwater anglers, is to land the grander. Its just harder for the guy that doesn't have an unlimited budget to be able to put it all together.

The next day Al, Frenchy, an old family friend Betsy Richardson there for the Wahine (women's) Fishing Tournament and myself, headed out of Lahaina for Honolulu. On the way home, in almost perfect calm conditions, Betsy caught a couple of nice thirty-pound Ahi.

A few days later Al caught a six hundred and fifty- seven pound blue marlin off of Honolulu, fishing alone.

Chapter 7

A Rio Return

A few days after Christmas, 1993, Mitch called me from Rio De Janeiro, Brazil. "Horizons" and "Tyson's Pride" were going back up to the Caribbean and he wanted to know if I'd be available for the trip north. I couldn't say either way immediately and asked him if I could let him know in a week or so. Mitch said, "No problem, give me a call." I asked how everyone was doing? He replied that they had a new engineer, deck hand, and cook, so he was trying to get organized. I also asked, "How are the cats doing?" Mitch said, "Hoby is getting heavy and Li'l Bloke has been missing since last August." They had no idea what happened to him. I was sorry to hear that. A week later I rang Mitch back and accepted the offer. The trip north from Rio should be fairly quick with the winds and currents pushing us all the way. The boats would be departing Rio the end of March or beginning of April '94.

Changes

When things are going well and you are enjoying yourself, remember and cherish those times. Personal and family problems looked to be putting a huge detour in our normal routine. Life's gear shifts can be something else to handle, but you have to go with the punches. This whole episode would remind us just how precious life really is.

A Rio Bummer

With all that was going on at home and the shop being so busy my decision not to go on the delivery from Rio to the lower Caribbean had been made. I called Mitch and advised him of the situation. He understood, wished me well, and told me they wouldn't be leaving for a few weeks so if I changed my mind, let him know. I always hate to miss a down-hill delivery, especially when you're going to end up in the Island of Grenada in the lower Caribbean. Oh well, there would always be another trip, or would there?

What's On The "Horizons"

Mitch would call periodically and give me progress reports. It looked as though the sportfisher would be heading for a major refit at the builder's yard in Florida, so "Horizons" would be doing short cruises in the Caribbean waters through mid December. After that "Horizons" would be heading for Florida and she would also be undergoing a major refit.

A few months before "Horizons" was to head back to Florida Mitch called to tell me that after "Tyson's Pride" arrived in Florida, the builder and owner got together to look into the costs of the rebuild. After the dust settled the owner had ordered a new boat. The rebuild looked as though it may cost close to a million dollars. Rumor had it that the builder, Merritt boat works, said they would give him a million on a trade. The new boat would cost nearly three million, so a deal was made on a new boat that was bigger than the last one by three feet. The only problem was that the boats had to be ready for a trip across the Atlantic Ocean next June to Madeira Island near the northwest tip of Africa. Mitch was going to get "Horizons" back to Florida just before Christmas '94 then he would go home to Australia for Christmas with his wife and his family. After he returned in January he would be one busy guy getting the "Horizons" rebuilt before the June deadline. He had asked me if I would be available to do the trip across the Atlantic on the "Horizons." I accepted the offer.

Which Two Items?

The end of winter and the spring saw my boat business as busy as it's ever been. The work wouldn't taper off until late September. We ran the boat over to Catalina Island a few times during the summer. On one particular trip to Avalon we were having dinner at the El Galleon restaurant. With each entree you could have the choice of any two items with your meal, example: potato and salad, etc. My wife, Linda and I were sitting in the middle of the restaurant. My chair was facing the walkway in from the front door. Linda was on my left and to see the walkway she would have to turn to her left a little bit. We were reading the menu, figuring what we would have for dinner. A beautiful Mexican girl, who usually worked there as a waitress, walked into the restaurant with a date. She had on a tight low-cut dress that made her breasts appear ready to pop out of the top of the dress. They were directed to the table straight across from my chair. As she started to sit down she bent over, and being a typical guy, my eyes were fixed. At the same time Linda, who was unaware of the situation and reading the menu, asked me which two items I wanted to have with my meal. When I didn't answer she looked up at me, then looked in the direction I was gazing. Immediately, she kicked me under the table, which finally got my attention. I looked at Linda and we both just started to laugh.

I had a good idea what Marty Robbins was thinking when he wrote his famous song "El Paso."

A First

My boat shop was swamped with projects when the local fishing started in late July. So what do fishin' addicts do when the fishing gets hot? Hang out the "Gone Fishin'" sign. The first day fishing on my boat the "Ghost Rider" this year was a two-day trip with Tracy Merrill. We had a late start, but it only took us a short time to catch our bait and head off to the Fourteen-Mile Bank. We didn't see a thing that afternoon and ended up at Dana Point for the night. At anchor, under the mesa cliff that marks Dana Point Harbor, Tracy barbecued up a great tri-tip for dinner.

We were up at 4:30 a.m. and off to the 277 spot via the Fourteen-Mile Bank. About six miles from the 277 we encountered the coldest water temperature of the day. We were both in the tower and he was sort of dozing off when I spotted his birthday present for the year, four sleepers off the port bow about a hundred yards ahead. I made sure it wasn't a dream and gave ol' Tracy a quick elbow, he jumped up and spurted "Wha..t." I said "I think it's your lucky day, look!" He almost jumped over the side getting to the cockpit to pull in the trollers, which made me laugh, and he was giving out orders, do this, do that! I, of course politely said, "Shut the @#&*! up! Just get up on the bow ready to cast." The fish were crossing our bow at about eighty yards, so I slowed and turned to port, wanting to approach them from up wind and give Tracy a shot so the fish

70

would be heading for the bait as he cast. We crossed behind the four fish, slowly turning to starboard so the fish would be crossing the bow from starboard to port and not be heading away from us. As soon as I had turned, I stopped the boat so the fish were heading to cross the bow at fifteen to twenty yards. The momentum of the boat would close the gap as the fish neared the bow area. At the same time Tracy cast a nice "greenie" mackerel from starboard to port, the bait landed about eighteen yards out at ten o'clock relative to the bow (the bow being twelve o'clock). As soon as the bait hit the water the four fish lit-up like a neon sign and all four did a beeline for the "greenie," a sight few people ever see! The fact that there were four fish made it a drag race for the bait. Often if there is only one fish, the marlin will not be interested, but when there are two or more marlin the competition aspect of nature kicks in.

Tracy was "bit" immediately and the fight was on. He had the fish on twenty-pound Ande Tournament line with a Penn 12 T reel. This fish looked to be around 140 pounds and was turbo charged. The fish hauled-ass and was greyhounding for the wild blue yonder. We quartered him for a short distance and then he sounded. A short twenty minutes later we wired him and since it was Tracy's first personal fish and the boat's first fish of the year we boated him instead of tagging.

At twenty knots Avalon was only about an hour away. We pulled into the crowded harbor at nine-fifteen Sunday, August 7, 1994. The line-up of boats waiting to be assigned a mooring clogged the fairway to the pier but we managed to get through. We weighed the fish in at Rosie's on the pier and found out that this was only the second marlin caught so far this year! There had been two swordfish caught on rod and reel, which is a hard way to catch a swordfish, so our fish was number four on the board. Tracy cleaned the fish on the way home, smoked all of it the next day and we consumed it all in a few weeks.

Needless to say the summer was fun with a few striped marlin releases and a lot of trips to Catalina Island. At the end of summer I did three tournaments at Catalina. The best we did this year was to have a large marlin spit the hook at the gaff. That fish would have easily placed in that tournament and I only missed winning the lottery by five numbers in a six-number lottery.

Tracy's Fish

Fish Oil and Water

Linda has been an avid sailor since way before we met back in the seventies. We have done a good number of regattas together, some short and some long, many off to distant places. In fact we were on the same boat on a good number of record-setting wins. The fact that I've fished longer than I've sailed has never really been a big deal in our relationship. She'd go sailing and I'd go fishing. The one thing about sailing is that it might be fun but you can't eat the trophies. Linda enjoys it and that's what's important.

A Lahaina Return 1994

When Al Bento called and invited me to fish the Lahaina tournament again this October I quickly accepted. Late in October I flew over to Hawaii where Al met me at the airport in Lihue, Maui. On the ride to Lahaina we stopped at the new discount store and bought the provisions for the tournament. I had been busy at work and home and was unable to help Al bring the boat over from Honolulu. This year's tournament was a lot of fun, but our fishing was dismal. Al tried every trick in the book, we could barely catch tuna for bait. "This stuff does happen," Al said. We did catch a thirty-five pound ono (wahoo) on the first day and going into the last day the ono was still one of the ten heaviest fish. By the end of the tournament the ono didn't even place in the ono division. Well, we had a great time and it sure beat the heck out of working. We took the boat back to Honolulu the next day after the awards banquet. Lahaina Yacht Club still made damn good ribs.

The Christmas

This Christmas was a lot of fun. We usually don't get into Christmas as much as some folks, since I'm usually off somewhere in the world on a job. This year however, we went to Linda's sister's place and had a ball. Her brothers, sister, mom, dad, nieces, nephews and close family friends were there. We stayed for a couple of days. On the way down to her sister's home we stayed at her brother Ed's home in Fallbrook,

California. They live on five acres in back of the Camp Pendelton Marine base where they are fairly secluded. This gives the two kids a lot of running room and they see a lot of wild life including deer, coyotes, snakes, rabbits, etc. We spent a warm evening in front of the fireplace with the whole family having dinner. Afterwards the kids were allowed to open their presents since they would be in Ramona Christmas eve. The next day we all headed down south to Ramona, for a family Christmas. Some were staying in Hotels, some at the house and a couple of us even stayed in the huge motor home they had out back. The turkey was cooking for the whole day and everyone was antsy to open up gifts. The wine was pouring and everyone was aglow. Dinner was great! Turkey, real mashed potatoes, yams, cranberry sauce, gravy, cooked onions, green beans, rolls, pumpkin and apple pie, what a meal. There was a special feeling in the air that year everyone was very close and happy. Even the kids got along, well. . . . sort of. After dinner Linda's mom and dad handed gifts out. Most of us stayed up later than we should have. No one bothered setting any alarms for the next morning. A country breakfast, a few games of boccie ball and we headed home. It was fun while it lasted.

Back To the Boat Shop

1994 turned out to be the biggest year I ever had, and every cent was earmarked for one bill or the other, funny how that always seems to work. We did five major rebuilds on three sportfishers, a large racing sailboat and a city fireboat so things were jumping. The winter and spring were just a blur, summer and fall went by in super-turbo mode.

Starting With A Bang

1995 started with a bang all right. The smoke from the New Years Eve fireworks wasn't gone before I was off on my first job of '95. The first month the shop was swamped again and we had two customers' boats to be delivered. One to La Paz and one back from Cabo San Lucas. At the same time I was getting ready to start work running "Desperado."

Chapter 8

Desperado Days

At the end of December '94 Scott Guenther, owner of the sport-fisher "Desperado," gave me a call and asked if I could recommend someone to run the boat in Mexico, starting in February. I told Scott that I didn't know anyone I could recommend to work for him, because, "You're way too damn picky!" He responded with a little hurt in his voice, "What do you mean!" We had a long discussion and as it turned out he made me an offer I couldn't refuse, but I'd need a couple of days to figure it out. Linda just about fainted! "You did what! What about your business, me, the house, the cats, etc." After a little work it appeared that it could be put together. I made a deal with my shop foreman to run the business. We could be in phone contact constantly if need be. I would be able to fly back home as needed to take care of home and business. The best part was Linda could come down as much as she wanted to, for R & R and I'd be able to make a couple bucks going blue marlin fishing. As it were I took the job.

"Desperado" is a super custom Viking 57, full tower, 2000 gallons of fuel, 1292's with turbos that could suck-start the Alaska pipeline, and capable of over thirty-five knots all day long. Her interior is perfect, a salon with two L-shaped couches covered with ostrich skin leather, two clear acrylic tables and a full galley. The twenty-seven-inch television is hidden until needed and then it is visible from the whole salon area. Along with the stereo in "surround sound" mode you feel like you're IN the movies that are playing on the VCR. Below forward the three staterooms are equipped with their own television, stereo, VCR, head (bath with shower) and air conditioner.

A couple of days before departure I began working on "Desperado." There were a lot of loose ends to take care of like stowing a whole cockpit of extra gear, and what seemed like ten thousand rolls of paper towels, (Scott said, "We'll use em'"). Tom and I said, "You can BUY them in Mexico!" Anyway there were a couple of hectic days before getting under way and finally we hit the road. Tom Powell had taken care of "Desperado" since we delivered the boat to California in 1989. Tom is an expert at maintaining a boat like this, but he does not have the opportunity to do a lot of deliveries because he maintains other boats and has a large family to feed and manage. Tom would go down to Cabo with us. He would commute back and forth to the various ports in Mexico, where the boat would be located, to do periodic boat detailing. This was Scott's idea since I did not have a lot of time to get to know all the systems and I would be on board in Mexico without a full-time deck hand.

We departed for San Diego at mid day on Valentine's Day, the wife was really happy about that! We headed for San Diego with a crew of four, Scott, Mike Volpe, Tom and myself. We would arrive in San Diego about midnight and since we were trying to establish a fuel usage curve we would be refueling in San Diego the next day. We arrived on schedule and were soon asleep. It had been a long few days getting the boat ready for the trip. In the morning even Scott didn't wake up early. We all rolled out of bed around nine a.m. After going out for breakfast we moved over to the fuel dock, filled up and departed midday.

The first couple days were fairly smooth and all we did on watch, besides engine checks, was watch the ocean water temperature go up. On the morning of the second day we started trolling. That night we had a hookup on top of the Uncle Sam Bank, located roughly midway between Turtle Bay and Magdalena Bay about sixty miles off of the Baja Coast in the Pacific Ocean. It was a big tuna but only a few minutes into the fight he jumped off.

The Thetis Bank just above Magdalena Bay was not very active. We proceeded to the

Morgan Bank, approximately one hundred miles southeast, half way between the bottom of Mag Bay (Cabo Lazaro) and the tip of the Baja Peninsula (Cabo San Lucas), where we had some good action. Approaching the bank we spotted a pack of birds off the starboard bow. Below the birds we spotted four feeders. Trolling over them we were "bit" immediately. Mike Volpe had a nice striper on, maybe a hundred and seventy pounds. The fish was working hard to spit the hook but Mike kept the line tight and worked the fish for about twenty minutes when all of a sudden he came unbuttoned. After that episode Scott decided to make lunch, today was "Desperado Dog" Day. So Scottso hauls himself into the galley and starts whipping up some "Desperado Dogs", which consist of hot dogs, tortillas and only Scott knows what else, but they tasted great. We trolled the same area for a couple of hours with not much luck. We finally pulled in the gear later in the afternoon and headed for Cabo San Lucas.

We arrived in Cabo San Lucas harbor to find that only one slip was open and that was only for the night. We found out the next day that there would be no slips available for a couple of weeks and since you needed to make reservations in Cabo for at least three months at a time to reserve a slip, we had a problem. We headed out for the mooring area, off of the long sand beach extending across the whole bay, eventually ending up moored just outside the "Office" restaurant. This was not a bad thing. This beach is a great swimming beach, the water is always warm and the surf during the season (November through June) is usually very small. Scott, being single, found that after a hard day of fishing all it took was a short swim into the beach and he was surrounded with lots of young ladies, sun bathing and drinking ice cold beer. The few days we were there we developed a great routine; Scott's friend Mike Volpe and myself, being the elder and more responsible persons that we are, took "Wahoo Juan's" ponga, the water taxi, into the beach. This way we could bring Scott a towel, shirt, hat, sunglasses, money, oxygen, etc. for a more comfortable and productive stay on the beach, after his swim in. We had this routine well rehearsed by the time we departed for La Paz a few days later. The fishing off Cabo had started to slow down a bit with the only productive area at that time being the Gordo Banks, up north inside the Gulf about twenty miles from Cabo.

We fished the Gordo on the way up to La Paz with just a couple of strikes. As we headed for the anchorage at Frailies, which is forty miles north of Cabo, we had a blue marlin come into the right short corner and gobble up the lure. This three hundred and fifty-pound marlin, came into the jigs from a forward direction, a bit unusual. Instead of tailing from the aft side of the jig, he was really lit. He hit the jig and jumped out of the water at the same time, making Scott jump because he was standing at the right corner taking a leak over the side when the fish came in. The rig the fish was on was a fifty-wide Penn International with fifty-pound Dacron line. The fish jumped twice by the boat and took off. Scott grabbed the rig and motioned to me to back down on the fish. This fish was moving out when all of a sudden the rod started to jerk violently. Apparently the fish had become tail wrapped and was jerking the line with his tail. After a minute or so of this the fish broke off. Dacron line makes it a bit tougher to fight these fish since the line has no stretch and breaks easier. Some Australian captains like to fish the larger rigs (130's) with Dacron. We proceeded to Frailes and anchored for the night. A great BBQ and off to LA LA Land after a long hard day of fishing. I guess if we worked as hard as we fished, we'd all be filthy rich!

The next day we headed for La Paz, eighty miles north of Frailes. We managed to nail a couple of twenty-five-pound yellow-fin tuna on the way. Because the weather was great we ran hard for the last forty miles into the Palmilla Marina at the entrance to La Paz Harbor. Our reservation was a great slip. It allowed us to refuel from the slip and gave us a great view of the Grand Canyon-type panorama across the Bay of La Paz. It was a spectacular unobstructed view of the sunset.

The next morning we refueled. Fuel man, "Gamma," was wrapped up like a lift operator at a ski resort. He had on a jacket, hat, gloves, and a scarf around his neck. There was a light northerly breeze coming out of the Gulf of California but we had on shorts, t-shirts and obviously thought the weather was more like a California summer than a La Paz winter. WE weren't cold! After checking in with the marina, doing our paperwork (necessary at every port in Mexico) and securing the boat, Scott and Mike headed for the airport. They'd be back!

Club De Atun O Quatro Amigos

Well it's ten p.m. Wednesday, March 15, 1995. ZZ TOP is playing on the CD player. It took all friggin' day to make the yacht "Desperado" transform, from a floating snow- ball (from all the dried salt water) to the sportfisher she is.

The last four days were unbelievable. Friday night El Jeffe (Scott Guenther) showed up with Larry, Moe, and Curly (Larry Kennison, Mike Blower, and Chris Dreyer). This group can not only pull on a rod they know what they are doing, on and off the boat! Scott Guenther is the owner of a very successful carpet manufacturing business, an avid angler and probably on the ten most wanted bachelor list. Mike "Lightest cocktail I've ever made!" Blower has been on seven teams who have caught swordfish on rod and reel. Larry Kennison, renown for being on the original team that created the world famous "GIGGLING MARLIN" restaurant in Cabo San Lucas. Living in Cabo, he had, and took the opportunity, to fish his butt off. Oh yes, these three distinguished gentlemen are Catalina Island Tuna Club members, of course. Chris Dreyer is Mike Blower's brother-in-law, owns a large landscaping business, has long hair and an earring (that keeps him out of the Tuna Club) and can reel in a thirty-pound yellowfin like it's water skiing.

Friday evening the group arrived from the airport in La Paz bringing all of their luggage, but of course, leaving the ever important cooler behind at La Paz International. After dinner at the Dinghy Dock restaurant we all hit the hay after a couple of cocktails Mr. Blower had done up for us, "Lightest cocktail I've ever made." If you were near an open flame, after a sip, your breath would blow your head off.

Saturday morning we are off bright and early for the reef north of Cerralvo Island.

No wind, smooth seas and sunny, a nice way to start the trip. After running hard for an hour or so we arrived at the area, twenty-five miles from La Paz. On the way out the boys were busy rigging all the tackle, etc. After a while we pulled in our first mahi. Things were not real stellar at this spot so we headed off for the "88" Bank, twenty miles southeast of Cerralvo Island. There the action picked up. By the time we pulled into Muertos anchorage for the night, forty miles south of La Paz, we had nabbed six mahi. The iridescent green, yellow and blue colors of a mahi-mahi are absolutely beautiful, it's too bad they are one of the best eating fish in the ocean. After the usual wash down and clean up, Scott barbecued up five huge baseball-sized filet mignons for dinner. With salad and a potato we looked like five basketballs with legs by the end of the meal. It had been a long day and it didn't take long for every one to sack out.

The next day we ran to Punta Arenas thirty miles to the south where we dropped the lines in and immediately snagged a nice mahi. About as fast we gaffed a fifteen-pound yellowfin tuna Scott angled. Early in the afternoon we arrived on the Outer Gordo Bank and waited for our first marlin. We were zipped a couple of times and once we had four fish in the lures behind the boat at the same time, but without any live bait drop backs, we didn't get hooked up. Around dusk we headed for the anchorage off of the Palmilla Hotel. Hors d'oeuvres were fresh yellowfin sashimi and dinner was fresh mahi-mahi and tuna, a healthy meal that all our bodies appreciated. Rock and roll was the order of the night as far as the mooring was concerned. A little breeze kept the chop slapping against the hull up forward which is where Scott's cabin is located. In the morning Scott looked like he had not slept very well from the noise keeping him awake all night.

Day three, Monday, March 13, off to the Gordo banks again. Sure is nice to go to fish instead of work on a Monday! Lines in and almost immediately we were zipped. An hour later zip number two. One more hour and we were "bit." Chris had a nice striped marlin on twenty-pound test Dacron. The fish jumped at least six times as he headed towards the middle of the Gulf. The fight seemed like it lasted longer, with all the maneuvering, and trying to keep the angler in the boat and in a position to be able to work the fish. But only twenty-one minutes later the 150-pound marlin was tagged and released.

A little while later marlin number two, again on twenty-pound Dacron, was also released. After the dust settled we had released two marlin and had in excess of twenty zips, a successful day, considering the conditions. There was twenty-five knots of wind from the north and six-foot seas. We backed down so hard on our first fish that we had over a foot of water on the back deck. This is why the aft-deck freezer with all of our frozen baits went out. That evening we anchored at Frailies. The well-protected anchorage allowed every one to get a good night's sleep. Even after a few fellow Tuna Club members dropped by for cocktails. Although there are only a few homes located in Frailies Bay, a group of Tuna Club Members were staying in one of these homes and spotted "Desperado" as she pulled into the anchorage. Being neighborly they jumped into their skiff and brought out a welcome package for the evening "happy hour." Late into the night, after a great barbecued tuna dinner you could hear across the bay, "Lightest cocktail I've ever made."

The fourth day we awoke (around nine) to a strong breeze from the north, where we were going, of course. We headed off the beach about ten miles and started to fish. After the lines were wet for an hour, we were bit and after a short fight, boated a nice thirty-pound yellowfin tuna. As we headed north the fishing stayed very consistent

"Desperado"

boating a fish, it seemed like, almost every hour on the hour. The boys' flight home was at 9:55 p.m. which translated into leaving for the airport around eight p.m. By four forty-five the breeze had settled in at twenty knots, seas, five feet and we were 43 miles from La Paz. Time to put ol' "Desperado" to work, so we took off at twenty-three knots and arrived at our slip in the Palmira Marina at six-thirty p.m. We took a lot of spray and a couple of times it seemed we were doing a crash dive in a submarine.... and the isinglass held! As the sun slid over the tabletop hills across the bay, we secured to the dock. Darkness fell just in time not to see the snow ball appearance the salt made of the boat.

The group had an hour to pack their gear and fish for the flight home and cook a great rib dinner. Since the cooler was still no where to be found, three foam coolers were purchased and soon they were all on their way to La Paz International.

Wednesday, March 15, I awoke to see the snowball from hell. Washing a boat with the water pressure in this marina is like pissing on the Great San Francisco Fire. After a bit of work "Desperado" was ready to do it again.

Thursday, March 16, the missing cooler arrived… It wasn't big enough for all the fish they had anyway!

On to Mazatlan

After I returned from a short trip to California Tom and I took off with "Desperado" for Mazatlan. The first day we trolled the eighty miles from La Paz, south to Frailes anchorage. Catching a couple of nice twenty-five pound mahi-mahi on the way. The ocean was flatter than a pancake that day and the only hope I had was that the conditions would hold for the next day. We anchored at five-thirty and after doing a complete engine room check, basically checking all the fluids (oil, water etc.) and getting the boat ready to run at twenty knots across the Gulf, we had another great BBQ.

Early the next day we departed for Mazatlan, the ocean was a mirror. The distance from Frailes anchorage to Mazatlan is one hundred and sixty-five miles and we planned to run at twenty knots, so we would arrive around five o'clock that evening. After running only a half an hour, we spotted a swordfish. Tom took over as I cast a live bait at the swordy just to have him sink out and disappear. Off we went and again about twenty miles later, Tom spotted a couple stripers sleeping on the surface. Once again we tossed a live bait at the fish but they did not seem to be very interested in the bait and boat combination plate.

About two-thirds of the way across and about a half mile away, we spotted a floating object, normally this would have fish under it, so Tom slowed down to trolling speed. Dropping in a couple lines we trolled by the object in hopes of catching some mahi-mahi. As we passed the float its appearance was a lot different than the other floats we had spotted in the gulf. Pulling in the lines we turned back toward the object to investigate. As we pulled up I snagged the float with a boat hook and brought it along side. It was wrapped with duct tape and plastic. Pulling out a knife and cutting the float open we found a bail of marijuana, packaged up nice and pretty. There must have been six or eight individually wrapped packages inside. We looked at this for about two seconds and high-tailed it out of there! All I knew is that this float, as valuable as it might be to some, spelled danger to us. In all the miles I have done on the oceans of this world I had never run across a float like that one. I've heard stories of other people running across stuff like that but it was a first for us.

The remainder of the trip was pleasantly boring. We arrived in El Cid Marina, Mazatlan, at five-fifteen. The marina was fairly empty of boats although we had a lot of help finding our slip from the marina personnel on the docks. Our mission here was to fish for swordfish for four or five weeks.

After a washdown we headed off for a bite to eat and found one of the nicest restaurants I've ever seen in Mexico, Sr. Peppers. The waiters were all dressed in tuxedos so we felt a bit underdressed when we walked in, in shorts. The food was excellent and the live music was great.

As it turned out, the boat only fished five days out of the month it was in Mazatlan. Business before pleasure and Scott was a busy boy at work that month. The only thing that came up was the fact Tom and I both became very ill after eating at a certain fast food restaurant. The quarter pounder with cheese was good but we think the water in the cola we drank may have gotten to us. I had a temperature of one hundred and four the day I went to the doctor at the El Cid Hotel. This doctor was great, spoke fluent English and had seen the symptoms many times. After a general check out he informed me that I needed three shots and a couple of prescriptions filled for antibiotics. I am not a shot man. The guy was good, I didn't even feel the needles, but I did feel the medicine because it burned like a son-of-a-bitch. The next day I felt much better but it took a week or so until I was back to normal.

Mazatlan is the largest and oldest seaport on the west coast of Mexico. It has spread-out to become a large city with tourism being the biggest business. The hotels line the beach from the shipping harbor, ten miles north, to the entrance to El Cid Marina. One other captain there gave me a sheet of paper that had six bar/restaurants with all of the times for happy hour. You could literally go from one happy hour to another from noon to four a.m. if you wanted to. The swordfishing was slow with only one fish being caught and only one other boat having a hookup while we were in Mazatlan. After a month in this place I was ready to go south. The trip southward to Puerto Vallarta, via Isabel Island, was smooth enough but the fishing really sucked. Two swordfish were spotted the day we departed Mazatlan but these fish spooked before we could approach. We managed to catch only two mahi-mahi on the way to Puerto Vallarta. In fact the fishing was lousy until we departed P.V. and arrived at the Bajo Bank twenty miles off the coast of the town of Manzanillo. Our anchorage at Isabel Island, the first night out of Mazatlan, was nice enough but after spotting a couple local longliners in the area we spent one day fishing there before heading for Puerto Vallarta. We trolled the whole day going to P.V. All we had was a couple strikes at Roca Corbetena sixteen miles outside the entrance to Banderas Bay, the twenty-mile deep bay where Puerto Vallarta is located.

The harbor in P.V. has been building up for the last few years and has become one of the most complete marina facilities on the West Coast of mainland Mexico. The marina is modern with a new haul-out facility and fuel dock. With the marina's proximity to the international airport (one mile away), Puerto Vallarta has become a popular year-round harbor. Because it's tucked in the back of Bandedras Bay, the harbor has become a desirable off-season hurricane hole. A spot for many yachtsmen to either leave their boats in a slip or in dry storage in the shipyard. While in Puerto Vallarta, Scott's friend John Paul (not Jean-Paul Richard) joined us. We did an oil change and refueled, not leaving a lot of time for shore leave before departing for Manzanillo. Being Easter time, known in Mexico as Semana Santa, the town was a madhouse, people everywhere. Semana Santa usually goes on for two weeks while everyone in Mexico celebrates Easter.

The next morning, after running hard for only an hour and a half, we covered the forty miles to where the ocean finally turned a clear blue, where we would start fishing. The day and conditions were perfect but the fishing was non-existent and as the daytime slipped by we decided to anchor in the cove off the beach at Club Med, Careyes. A late arrival in the cove dictated a late departure the next morning, after a swim and checking out the scenery. The cliffs along the coastline at Careyes average a couple hundred feet in height with homes scattered around the surrounding hills over-looking the three bays that make up Careyes. The Club Med is located in it's own bay and is very secluded, with a great private beach.

After departing Careyes, we trolled south and as the westerly winds started to come up early in the afternoon we found ourselves trolling over the Bajo Bank. When we were on top of the second high spot we had a blue marlin come in and nail the lure on the left rigger. The wind came up to twenty-five knots and the seas were four feet and building. The fish went off to our port side, greyhounding for what seemed to be forever. The reel was a Penn International twenty with twenty pound Dacron line. Our guest John Paul was the angler. I turned the boat and quartered the fish for a few minutes until we had steadied-up the line-to-fish-to-angler relationship. Afterwards we played him off the port corner. This fish was in the one hundred ninety-pound range. Just fine for the conditions and the tackle we had him on. This blue marlin made a good show of it, jumping, turning, spinning and, when he was close to the boat, doing a couple power runs on the surface with his bill out of the water. After thirty minutes we were able to wire the fish and then release him in good condition. John was one happy camper, this was his first twenty-pound tackle blue marlin and being Dacron line made that even better. Considering the conditions and all, he had earned it. After all the excitement we ran into Manzanillo and anchored behind the Las Hadas Marina just off the beach at the Las Hadas Hotel.

The next morning I ran the skiff into the harbor to check on our reservation for a spot to med-moor (setting the bow anchor and then stern tying to a dock or pier). The personnel seemed like they were still on Semana Santa (Easter holiday). They directed us to a spot that had just been vacated. We anchored and backed in. Besides the anchor not holding, the other boat coming back and wanting their spot back, the marina officer being anywhere but near his office or a radio, the transom almost smacking the dock, the owner and guest needing to get to the airport soon, everything was JUST FINE! The marina officer finally came back over the radio and told us that he had made a mistake. He had assigned us another vessel's spot and that he had no other spots for a few days. Sure glad we had reservations! By this time Scott was fed-up with all the B.S. John Paul had to get home so he took off for the airport. Scott, "Desperado" and myself headed for the new marina at Ixtapa, one hundred and eighty miles south of Manzanillo. Well at least we had a good night's sleep last night.

This change of plans really screwed up the works. We had people coming in to Manzanillo and all would have to change their airline reservations. There would be extra charges and hassles for reserving flights to Ixtapa less than two weeks before flying, oh well! Scott just took it in stride, same old thing, when it looks like it is going to work, it doesn't. Scott also had to be home for work and that meant a complete reshuffle of his air reservations.

It Didn't Ixtapa Us From Going!

We took off for Ixtapa and for the first part of the day we fished. As the day progressed the wind came up hard, thirty-five knots plus by late afternoon. We pulled in the lines and bumped the speed up to fifteen knots and started to look for a spot to pull into for the night. Yeah, sure! We pulled into a cove called Lizard Bay and found the seas breaking around the rock that protected the harbor. The swell wrapped around the rock and reformed behind it and then built until it broke in the shallow water off the beach. This highly recommended anchorage sucked. Scott just looked at me and said, "Well, how about chili instead of BBQ'd steaks tonight?" Off to Ixtapa.... We re-figured our ETA and decided to up the speed to twenty knots. The extra fuel capacity that Scott had built into the boat paid off again. We would be in Ixtapa around midnight. As the sun went over the yard arm and behind the clouds that were building behind us, I thought of how similar this coast was to the coast off of Big Sur, California: hazy, cloudy and windy. Only here it was eighty-five degrees. As we neared the Ixtapa area, still forty miles to the south, the wind laid down, the seas flattened out, the clouds became more spotty, the moon came out and the water temperature went from seventy-seven to eighty-three degrees in about five miles distance. The last forty miles were smooth as a babe's butt, and we're not talking baby's butt.

We arrived at Ixtapa Harbor entrance at midnight. This harbor was relatively new and its exact location was a mystery to both of us. I knew where the harbor should be, after talking to a few of the other boats we had crossed paths with on the way down. We also knew the entrance was deep but fairly narrow. As we neared the area where we had been told the harbor was located, it stuck out like a sore thumb on the radar. We neared the entrance and realized there was a five-foot swell running which would add a little zest to our first entry into Ixtapa Harbor at midnight. The entrance had two sets of floating red and green lights, one set outside the entrance maybe thirty feet and the second set inside the harbor a hundred feet. This made lining up the entrance a lot easier.

As we snuck up to the entrance all looked fine but it was obvious that we would have to go in with more power due to the swell running. I ran the throttles up so we had a reasonable amount of headway and followed a wave into the entrance. After everything else that had happened that day I jokingly told Scott I was going to need a drink after we arrived. As we entered the first set of lights, the bow pulled a bit to starboard, and for the moment it took to steady the boat out, Scott's pucker string, I believe, tightened a little. Then I'm sure he strained it when I told him the bottom on the depth sounder went from twenty-five feet to three feet as we entered the jetty! Hard to say, he didn't utter a sound, but I think he stopped breathing for a second or two. Well, as they said when I had a little boat built a good number of years ago and something would go wrong during the construction, "It ain't my boat!" Of course I said that to myself because I didn't need a gaff run through me before I had that arrival drink. We entered the harbor and the depth sounder read seventeen feet. We later found out that due to all the turbulence at the entrance to the harbor, the silt would show false readings on most depth sounders. A few minutes later we were secured to a dock, power plugged in and the arrival festivities began.

In the morning we were assigned another slip and moved to it first thing. Scott had made airline reservations over the SSB radio through his office for a flight out at midday.

Cleanliness Is Next To Godliness

Ixtapa Marina is a beautiful, well built marina. The docks are as nice as I've seen anywhere. The town of Ixtapa is a model city, one off the cleanest in Mexico. The town of Zihuatanejo three miles to the south is almost as nice. "Geneva M" from Long Beach and "Gene's Machine" from Cabo San Lucas were here. I noticed that "Gene's Machine" was fishing with 130 Penns. Some may have thought that a little over kill, but after seeing the fish that were here I think he was on the right track. Some day those boys will be ready when the big one comes in. A few years later, they would place in the top of three tournaments in a row and win almost a million dollars in the process.

The marina is located where a river mouth empties into the ocean. With the river still flowing through the marina you can venture up the river in a skiff, through a golf course behind the marina. In the golf course the river divides into smaller legs as it winds though the course. On one island, in the middle of the course, are a bunch of logs, problem is they aren't logs, they're crocodiles. This explains the signs in the marina that warn the public of the crocodiles and of course there are no professional boat bottom cleaners here. All of that can be done in the clear waters off of Isla Grande, a couple miles north of Ixtapa. One particular crocodile, Pancho, regularly swims into the marina and hangs out near some of the sportfishers that throw fish to him. It is amazing how fast a crocodile can move. I've watched Tony, the captain on "Gene's Machine," pull Pancho's tail, cautiously! Pancho could easily jump up on the dock but he seems tame enough to just take the fish thrown to him and watch the people watching him.

"Desperado" would now be based out of Ixtapa for about six weeks and would start fishing the following weekend. After Scott departed, the boat had a good clean up and preparations for the following week of fishing began. The tackle would be fifty-pound

Pancho

and higher since the word was out that the blue marlin and large yellowfin tuna had shown up. I found that to be very true that afternoon when I took a cab into Zihuatanejo to clear our papers. I was walking up to the Port Captain's office and observed a Mexican fisherman riding his bike from the pier. In the three-wheeled bike with a three-foot square basket between the front wheels were three rods and one yellowfin tuna weighing, he said, one hundred and fifty-two KILOS! Over three hundred pounds, he was one happy fisherman. Later we would find that the ponga fishermen, pongas being small open boats powered with outboard motors, had better results with the tuna than the larger boats. It seemed that they could run through the schools of porpoise into the tuna schools and would not spook the tuna like the larger boats would. You'd find these pongas right with the fleet forty miles out to sea!

Scott, John Paul and Mike Volpe flew into town a week later. The next day we departed for fishing at five-thirty. The area where we were headed was thirty-seven miles off the coast. We ran fast for an hour and set the gear about twenty miles from Ixtapa. Heading for the 1090 spot, we found no signs of life, birds, porpoise or tunas. As we neared the one-mile mark on the radar to the center of the 1090 spot we had a zip on the center rigger but it didn't stick. A few minutes later as we neared the center of the spot a blue marlin, weighing probably four hundred and fifty-pounds, hit the left rigger. When the slack out of the rigger tightened up, the rig started to peel reluctantly. The drag may have been too tight. The fish jumped twice and blew the rig apart. The Dacron line snapped and the fish greyhounded off to our starboard side, he was stung. As he took off he spooked another blue that jumped on the outside of him away from us. I slowed the boat for only a moment when it appeared that we were bit and when the marlin jumped off I ran the boat back to trolling speed.

As this was going on, four more blues came into the jigs behind the boat. Well, we thought there were four. The two fish on the left side were going after the left short corner and the other "two" appeared to be heading for the right rigger. The outside of the two fish I spotted going towards the right rigger had his dorsal up, was lit up and dead on the lure on the right rigger. The other fish just behind and inside appeared to be sounding since his tail was the only thing visible....

As I watched all this happening in just a matter of seconds, it hit me that there were not two fish on the right rigger but one BIG fish that was turning in towards the lure. He gobbled the lure like Wimpy on a hamburger. We were bit and bit good. He took off greyhounding aft from right to left. Then he turned and took off to our right in a straight line as if going down a runway. This run lasted only a few minutes. Meanwhile Scott grabbed the rod while John hooked Scott up with a belt. Soon he would need a harness. This is the time you wish you had a one-thirty rig and a real fighting chair.

Our Rybovich chair was in California in the garage. 'Bet Scott brings that next time he sends the boat down here!

Twelve feet was the estimated distance between dorsal and tail. An hour into the fight and the fish had only come up once at the start. It is still my contention that after the first run the fish hurt itself, probably a heart attack and the rest of the first hour it was dying. The fish seemed to be circling and sounding. Scott estimated the fish was 150 yards out, which wasn't bad. He also thought he had maybe 600 yards of line since it was fifty-pound Dacron. I mentioned that I thought the fish was dead and Scott said he could still feel the fish moving. After another thirty minutes, another 150 yards, and a lot of discussion, Scott tightened the drag a bit to try and slow the fish's sounding. By now Scott was sitting in a portable chair. He was getting a good work out from the fish, dead or alive.

The fish kept sinking down and finally when Scott thought he was 400 yards down he tightened the drag some more. It was time for go or no go. Finally Scott agreed that the fish was dead. The sea conditions were very smooth so we started to plane the fish up. I'd move the boat forward slowly, get a bit of angle on the fish, then stop and briefly back down so Scott could get a small amount of line in. Doing this while slowly turning seemed very effective. At first we could only get a couple of inches at a time. An hour later we were getting sometimes up to fifteen feet. After three hours we had gained maybe a hundred yards back. This process was working well and after a few hours we were only one hundred and fifty yards out from the fish. I was real glad we had such smooth conditions.

As the fish neared the last fifty yards it all of a sudden seemed like it was getting heavier. With fifty-pound Dacron line we had to be delicate to win this fish. Five hours into the fight and we were less than two hundred feet from the leader. Scott was only able to get a few inches at a time and he had to tighten the drag more to keep the line he had won back. Scott was a beat puppy and was now resting the rod on the covering board, which made the fish illegal for any record. The planing was not as effective as it was earlier and we were barely moving the boat. We were ready to wire the fish when Scott pulled the rod up to try and get another inch or two, when the Dacron line gave out. The line broke at the double knot. It was quiet for a couple minutes but we got over it soon. It figures that with two fifty-pound rigs and three eighty-pound rigs the big fish always take the small rigs. We ran back into Ixtapa. Scott slept like a rock that night. He didn't even dream of the fish that could have weighed eight hundred to over a thousand pounds. Big fish need big tackle. This fish would have been the largest fish of this Mexico trip by at least five hundred pounds, oh well!

The four of us went to the airport to fly back to California. Tom had arrived to detail the boat for the few days I'd be gone. When we arrived at the airport we found they only had three seats. Boy, were we all unhappy about this. As it went Mike Volpe volunteered to stay and fly out the next day. Mike ended up having his wife fly down, stayed for ten days and had a great time.

The next weekend Scott, his lady friend Liz, Mitch and Laura Mitchell were flying in for a three day stay. With Mike and Sue Ellen already here we were all in for a fun weekend. I flew back to Zihuataneao a couple of days before the weekend to help Tom get the boat ready, since he would be leaving before the guests arrived. Mitch and Laura flew in from Miami. They were ready for a holiday, since being in the middle of a major refit on "Horizons" in Florida. They hadn't had a day off since the end of January. Between the pool, barbecue, fishing, and a couple of old movies on board, everyone had the time of their lives. Mike Volpe even made one of his famous Italian dishes one night. It was delicious and even if I did have gas for two days afterwards it was worth it. Scott, Liz, Mike and Sue Ellen flew out together, Mitch and Laura stayed for one more relaxing day by the pool.

Mitch and I talked about the upcoming trip to Madeira on "Horizons." He said the departure date was still around the fifteenth of June. He also mentioned that the gameboat, "Tyson's Pride," would be shipped over to Palma, Mallorca, on the ship "Dock Express." She'd return to Florida the same way in October. I asked what this would cost and he said, "Plenty, around a thousand dollars a foot each way!"

"Desperado" would be slip-side for a couple of weeks since Scott would be in Europe on a business trip. For a few days Linda flew down with some friends of ours, Dr.

Dr. Richard Daniels & Mike

Richard Daniels and his wife Camille, and did we have a good time! I basically took a couple days off, we lounged at the pool, took the skiff to Isla Grande for lunch and a swim, out to Zihuataneao for dinner one night, and I barbecued one night onboard. The few days we all had together were great, we still talk about it.

We fished a couple of days more in Ixtapa but the work load at Scott's business, combined with other commitments, had us heading for Cabo by the end of May with a delivery crew. The weather routing service we subscribed to, verified our weather fax maps that there was a tropical disturbance along the coast near Acapulco heading northwest toward Ixtapa. The service told us to wait until the next morning to depart for Cabo and if the weather was clear by nine-thirty go ahead and depart, if the weather was cloudy call them back and don't depart. As it was we had a tremendous lightning and rainstorm that night. By nine-thirty the next morning the weather was perfectly clear. We departed.

We released four blue marlin on the trip to Cabo San Lucas, one in the two-seventy range. One fish straightened the hooks when the eager angler tightened the drag too much, that fish was four-fifty. The boats in Cabo were starting to thin out a bit with the end of the safe weather season and the onset of the hurricane season. "Desperado" had the first slip on "K" dock and only went out of the harbor once for a rooster-fishing trip with Charlie Johnson, a friend of the owner's. On that trip we returned early to the dock when one of his guests became a bit seasick. A few days later Scott and Mike Volpe flew into town and we departed the next morning for Newport Beach, California. We arrived in Newport three days later.

Coast to Coast

The week after "Desperado" arrived home was as busy as it gets. Home, business, bills, and preparing to fly to Ft. Lauderdale, Florida, to join "Horizons" for the trip to Madeira Island off of Africa.

Chapter 9

Madeira

I flew into Ft. Lauderdale a couple of days before we were to depart for Madeira. "Horizons" was at Pier Sixty-six on the inland waterway side of the main dock. Behind her was the 167-foot "Jefferson Beach" and across the inland waterway were "Neninka," at 130 feet, with the "Gallant Lady" in front of her. The boats in Ft. Lauderdale amaze me because they always make quite a statement. There were a lot of things still on the list before we could depart. It was a very busy time. "Horizons" had just gone through a major refit and looked absolutely beautiful. Merritts had done the main salon over and it looked like a million bucks, in fact I was told that the rebuild cost about that. The boat had two sets of stabilizers installed. Which cost her a couple thousand gallons of fuel storage. She now would hold around twenty two thousand gallons instead of the twenty-five thousand gallons she used to carry. The main project that needed to be completed before departure was stowage of all kinds of gear and parts. What a job, eventually we were ready to depart.

Across The Pond

A few nights before our departure the owner and some of his friends had dinner with the crew aboard "Horizons." Don Tyson seemed to be very pleased with the results of the refit, at the same time the crew was able to put together a first-class dinner. Mark, the chef, was able to put his talents to the test and also had an opportunity to properly break in the newly modified galley.

The night before we departed, the crew had a great dinner at the restaurant at Pier Sixty-six where the boat was moored, and believe this, we all went to bed fairly early for a change.

By mid morning we had shoved off from the dock and were under way. We were waiting for the Seventeenth Street causeway bridge to open so we could depart Ft. Lauderdale for our first stop, Horta Harbor, Faial Island, in the Azores. The bridge finally opened and off we went, well at least through the bridge. As soon as we had

Captain Mitch

cleared the bridge the engine slowed and suddenly stopped. The bow anchor is always down a couple feet when the boat is in any harbor. This is done in case of any emergency so we would be able to stop the boat. We finally put this theory to the test, down went the hook. The boat actually ended up on the inshore side of the fairway off of a couple of ships that were berthed along the wharf. Ahead of us off our starboard bow was the "Roro Runner" and off of our starboard stern was the "Orion." Both ships seemed to be small coastal freighters, probably working the Bahamas or Caribbean. There was more than enough room for us between them if the wind were to shift and put us alongside the wharf. As it was the wind direction held and we just hung parallel to the ships and wharf. The transmission had blown a gasket and would be repaired and operational in fifteen minutes. We called the port authorities and told them of our situation, they said to keep them advised. When the gasket let go we lost almost all of the transmission fluid into the isolated engine sump. Our Australian engineer "Splitpin," (Mark James), assured both Captain Mitch and myself that we had more than enough spare fluid for the entire trip to Madeira

Adrian, Captain Mitch, Mike

Chef Mark Gagliardi, Yellow Fin, 1st Engineer Splitpin

and back. The fluid in the sump would be pumped into our used oil storage tank until it could be disposed of at a proper facility.

As we were waiting to effect repairs and get under way I heard the Coast Guard on channel 16 VHF ask local boaters to be on the lookout for a small airplane. It had taken off from Ft. Lauderdale and had apparently crashed off the coast approximately five miles. They also gave a position where they thought the plane went down. I plotted the coordinates and sure enough we would be heading over that area after we departed the harbor.

Peter and Laura Mitchell are the Captain and organizer of "Horizons," while Adrian is the long-time steward on board. For this trip a second engineer and myself as Delivery/backup Captain/ Navigator are brought aboard to help round out the crew. Laura would be flying to Madeira, via England, and would meet us when we arrived. For this trip, the crew would be Mitch, Adrian (steward), Mark James ("Splitpin" engineer), Mark (chef), backup engineer Bob Payne and myself. With repairs finished we were off to find an airplane while heading for the inside corner of the Bahamas at the north west corner of Little Bahama Bank. We had the binoculars out but all we spotted looking for the plane were all the other craft looking for the same plane. To this day we don't know if the plane or people were ever found.

Around eight p.m. that evening we rounded the way-point off of Little Bahama Bank and changed our course for the great circle route to Horta in the Azore Islands 2,635 miles away. This course would take us thirty miles north of Bermuda which was good for a couple of reasons: one, if we needed to stop for any purpose, Bermuda has everything and two, we would be out of the Bermuda Triangle by a couple of miles (facetious).

Middle of the Atlantic Ocean

The rain that we had the last days in Ft. Lauderdale slowly let up to beautiful skies with warm days. Besides having a glitch in our new GPS navigation system, everything was going smooth including the seas. The first morning out we landed a thirty pound wahoo and later had another one on that was close to fifty pounds. Three days before we arrived at the Azores we caught a yellowfin tuna weighing in at probably one hundred pounds. Boy that tasted good, and Mark now had all the fresh tuna he would need for the first part of the time they'd be in Madeira. The trip to the Azores was boring which can be construed as good, very little wind or seas all the way over. We did spot and pick up a lot of loose floats with radar reflectors. These are small metal shapes that will return a radar signal. They had been floating free for some time. Most of these floats had probably broken away from longline nets. A lot of free time was spent getting the boat ready for the arrival and all of the guests that would constantly be aboard for the duration of the time "Horizons" would be in Madeira.

Azore Arrival

We arrived in Horta harbor on July 7, 1995, at about six p.m. that evening. We had just enough time to tie up to our assigned spot, a side-tie with the Green Peace vessel, "Moby Dick". After they realized that we were not commercial fishermen and found we released most of our fish we all had an arrival beer and things were fine.

That evening we went out with a few old friends we met on the wharf. Yes, Vern was standing on the wharf when we tied up. He was working for the season on a

Horta Harbor

game boat called "Double Header." Not only was Vern here but he was working with his old friend, "Big Al." They'd gone out fishing one day getting ready for the season, "warmin up" as Vern put it, and released two fish, both around eight hundred pounds. They'd be fishing with two Captains during the season, first with Don Merton and later with Didier Armand.

Vern told us that during the 1994 season they had a good number of large fish on, but one fish was a giant, he called it "Mongo" and they even had a gaff shot. They stuck the fish and the fish straightened the 20" stainless gaff! They thought it a world record

Fueling

for sure. Well, before this season Vern had a new titanium gaff made 21" which is super lightweight, six pounds, just in case he gets another shot at "Mongo."

Black Sand Beach

Our Azore-style dinner was great, a local version of beef and potatoes. We had to get up early to move the boat to another wharf to fuel so I crawled back to the boat to get some rest before morning.

Wake up was early and enough of the crew responded so we could move the boat to the other wharf. Our agent had the fuel arranged early. We were topped off and back at the other wharf well before noon, not bad figuring we took on 8,660 gallons of fuel! That afternoon Mitch rented a car and we took a drive around the island of Faial. We always leave someone on the boat and we also invited a couple of the people next door to go with us. Faial is a very clean and well kept island. Although we were only gone for a few hours, we were able to see a good bit of the island.

Since the recent volcanic eruptions on the Island of Hawaii covered the black sand beaches, I had not seen another black sand beach, until the one on the Island of Faial.

It is customary to paint the name and a picture of the boat you're aboard on the wharf. If you don't do this it is considered bad luck. I was assigned this task and did a white

background with the blue boat in the middle, of course by the time I was finished everyone had signed their names and added their own little touches.

Last Leg To Madeira

We departed from Horta on July 9, and enjoyed a very flat trip to Madeira, seven hundred miles to the southeast. The passage took only three days and change. Looming out of the low overcast we finally spotted the vertical cliffs of the West End of the island of Madeira. Anywhere from three hundred to almost a thousand feet high, the cliffs would vary as we neared the island and started to round the southern side. Above the cliffs were green hills and meadows, with small towns spotted along the way as we headed for Funchal, the main town of the island. A couple of miles from Funchal the cliffs reach a height of almost two thousand feet with their base at the ocean's edge. The fishing this season would be best just a few miles off the coast in over five thousand feet of water.

We arrived on July 12, around noon, 3,370 miles from Ft. Lauderdale. By the time the hook was set and the large skiff was in the water I was requested to go out to the gameboat, "Tyson's Pride," a mission to look forward to. I thought it would have been special to just observe the fishing here. As we zipped out to "Pride" in the "Horizon's" large inflatable skiff, I looked back at the "mother ship" "Horizons" that brought us across the Atlantic and had a few quick thoughts on how good the ocean had been to us this time.   When I arrived Captain Tim Hyde introduced himself and the crew, Terry Robinson, who I met on the trip to Vitoria, Brazil, a few years ago on the old "Pride," and Australian Rick Thistlewaite, who has fished a lot of years with the best on the reef "down under." I soon realized that there were no guests, and found that I was the angler for the rest of the day, great! The guests had elected to stay ashore this day and "Prides" crew were going fishing, guests, or not.

New Tyson's Pride & Horizons, Madeira 1995

"Pride" was using a bait and lure combination system. They would troll four rods. The two lines in the riggers were sewn baits and the two lines on the corners were lures. While I was in Madeira the baits had most of the action but not all. They fish late here and we departed the grounds just before dark, without having one fish come up in the jigs, oh well, I had a good time anyway! On our ten-minute run to the harbor I asked Captain Tim if he would mind if I video taped the fishing the next few days with their camera. He thought that was a good idea and the following day I was ready to go. That evening Tim pulled out the camera, tapes, quick charger, etc. He and I went over procedures, checked everything out and it seemed to be in working order. The camera was not new and didn't have a gyro- stabilizer, but we'd make it work. I've done camera work for Disney, ESPN and for Channel Sea TV, all for on-the-water events, so I was looking forward to putting that experience to work.

This evening went as expected, getting the boat ready for the owners and guests. It did not take long. On the trip across the Atlantic the entire crew had attacked the "hit-list" of jobs with a vengeance and a very large portion of those were scratched off by our arrival.

A few other boats were here from different countries. "Chunda," is a nice 44-foot Garlington from Texas, owned by Stewart and Nickie Campbell, captained by Barkey Garnsey, with mates Spencer Stratton, Charles Perry, and soon-to-be an American citizen, their four-legged mascot, "Whiskers" Campbell. These guys are known as "The over the hill gang" but don't let that fool ya. "Chunda" is painted all white and built to fish, with as few extra systems as possible to spend more time fishing and less time maintaining, especially when the boat sits in storage during the off season.

"Captivator" is a Jim Smith design owned by Mike Day with Captain James Barnes, Ken Jones and Bob aboard. The 165-foot "French Look II" from France with her 41-foot custom G&S gameboat, "French Look III" aboard piggyback style, is one serious program. Owner Jean Paul Richard, who owned the 46-foot Merritt "French Look" we fished in 1989 in Cabo San Lucas, is a six-time world record holder, the largest line class being sixteen-pound test. He has one two-pound sailfish record, two four-pound sailfish records (Atlantic and Pacific), one four-pound striped marlin record, one eight-pound black marlin record, and one sixteen-pound Atlantic blue marlin record. He set all of these records before the new boat was finished. They had an awesome year last year in Madeira and surely are not finished with the record book. The boat and program were organized by Captain Mitch and Captain James Roberts a good number of years ago. The refit of the Louisiana oil boat was a monstrous task that took almost five years to complete. "French Look II" was listed as one of the one hundred largest yachts in 1995 by Power and Motor Yacht magazine. Captain James Roberts and crew have quite a program. From all the reports they seem to be doing a great job with the boats and the fishing. As of this printing Capt. James and crew have moved on to another program.

Another impressive boat, from Italy, was "Americana," a 55-foot Buddy Davis.

"Pesca Grossa" with Captain Kevin Nakamaru, commuting from Kona, Hawaii, was also catching their share of the fish.

Of course there are five or six local boats including "Margarita" with Captain Roddy Hayes who has been fishing the area for quite a few years. Roddy has made Madeira famous, being the original serious Captain and game boat here.

A lot of the serious world class fisherman were here. Mitch introduced me to Peter B. Wright who skippers "Duyfken" on the reef in Australia. It is said that Peter has caught more Granders than anyone. A few years ago his team landed three granders in one day. Peter is now a strong advocate of tag and release.

"Tyson's Pride"

The new "Tyson's Pride" is immaculate. The boat is spectacular inside and out, Merritt had done it again. This boat seemed a bit more elegant inside and the exterior simple, effective and gorgeous. The transom was of course varnished teak with a gold leaf name. The logo on the transom was new, the old "Pride" did not have a logo, just the name. The logo is "the" chicken riding a marlin, I liked it. It was explained to me that the chicken was an original logo of Don's company. The logo seemed to show that one of the worlds most serious fishing programs had fun.

This reminded me of an old friend, Roy Disney, who a few years ago used an old original cartoon character of a cat to name his racing yacht, "Pyewacket."

Mark, our chef, made a delicious dinner for the crews of both boats. By the time the detailing was completed for "Pride's" side-tie we were all ready for a good meal and a

night's rest. The next morning we headed out with guests George and Betsy Matthews (President of IGFA and owner of the Breakers Hotel in Palm Beach, Florida), also aboard was their daughter Kelly. We trolled the same area as the day before for a good number of hours, in fact it was soon lunchtime with no action as yet.

As the ladies were making lunch Tim spotted a fish coming in under the jigs. The fish went across from our left looking aft to our right and went back to the baits trolling behind the jigs. This was one of the biggest fish I've ever seen. As I turned the camera from "standby" to "on" the fish came into the right bait and sucked it down, the battle had begun. The ladies came out to see what was happening, as the fish was freight training through the water behind the boat. As this was going on the boys cleared the cockpit. The fish was magnificent, Rick shouted in Australian, "She's a bloody Grander for sure, mate!" The fish stayed fairly close to the boat because Tim was backing down fairly hard.

In fifty minutes or so the fish was near the boat and we had a real good look at her. The consensus was that she was over a thousand pounds. This was the biggest fish the angler, George, had ever fought and would be the first fish for the new "Pride." The decision was made to boat the fish. After an hour and a half the great fish was along side, close enough for Terry to wire. He found it had to be done with some finesse or he'd be over the side with the fish. The first few attempts to wire this fish were unsuccessful, Terry had to drop the leader more than once. The third time Terry was able to get the fish around to the starboard side of the boat. Rick was able to set the first gaff, and soon thereafter the second gaff was in and the fish subdued.

Next, get the fish in the boat. This was not an easy task even on a large Merritt like "Pride." Using everyone possible we pulled the fish into the cockpit. With his head lying on the entry to the main saloon and his tail hanging out the back, we ran into the harbor at Funchal. Since both boats are in constant radio contact the crew of "Horizons" knew the "Pride" had landed the marlin. "Horizons" was readying the boat boom and her electronic scale for the weigh-in. Because the fish did not appear to be a record, we wouldn't have to weigh it on shore. "Pride" backed into the starboard side of "Horizons." The loop was slipped over the tail and as the fish slid out the transom door, it looked to be a giant. Split hoisted the fish up until she cleared the water. Mitch pushed the button on the scale. The scale ran up to 995 pounds, five shy of a grand, not a bad fish for a beginning.

"Horizons" cat, (looking like a football with legs), Hoby, was standing on the top deck and spotted the fish hanging from the boom and must of thought she'd died and gone to heaven, boy was she licking her lips.

The marlin was taken into Funchal and given to the local hospital and orphanage. That night during a great dinner with the guests on "Horizons," the one question George asked was if we thought Don would be upset that George had broken-in "Pride." Everyone knew that would not be a problem, in fact Don would be excited about this fish.

The next day was ladies day. Betsy and Kelly were the anglers. Again about midday we were "bit" by a nice sized blue marlin, it was Kelly's turn and she worked the rod and reel like an old pro. Tim masterfully maneuvered "Pride" to help the angler with the fish. Within an hour she had gotten a release on a six hundred fifty-pound fish!

That evening a group of us went into the inner yacht harbor where the waterfront is lined with restaurants and had dinner. While going in we noticed "French Look II" was heading in to weigh a fish, we waited to see what she had. They had taken the refrigeration repairman, Larry Beard, out fishing in the afternoon and had hooked up a real "slob." The fish died so they weighed it in and gave it away to the locals. The fish weighed in at 1,203 pounds, nice fish!

The next day the Robinsons were supposed to fly in and fish while the Matthews were departing for home, but the Robinson's G-2 jet had a small problem, delaying their arrival by a day. Tim told us to be ready to be the anglers, Mark, Split, and myself were on board when we headed out the next day. The morning was again fairly slow and as we slipped into the afternoon it looked as though things would not get any better. While rotating turns on the rods, a few minutes after my time on the right two rigs started, Tim spotted a large fish under the right bait that soon came up for a bite. I was in the chair and in no time had the 130 Penn cranking like mad. This fish was stubborn and was heading out to sea fairly quickly. She'd get near the boat and just keep digging in with her head down all the time. The first time Rick wired her she pulled him around the covering board from left to right like a rag doll. He slammed so hard on the back covering board cushion that I thought he'd broken something. Anyway, the fish was stubborn but we finally were able to release her after an hour and a half fight. Both Rick and Terry figured the fish at nine hundred pounds.

Later that evening we went to an outdoor bar along the waterfront in the marina called Bar-o-Barrilihno. Our waiter Marco served us up a few cold ones as the various boat crews told tales of their day. A lot of the stories, could, by some in some places, be considered far-fetched, but with the reputation of the people, the boats and the fish located in Madeira, that would never happen.

The next day Jim and Donna Robinson along with Al and Roy Merritt arrived. They had flown to Madeira on the Robinson's G-2 Gulfstream jet via Bermuda and the Azores. Jim and Donna were building their second Merritt Boat, a beautiful 75-foot sportfisher named "Can't Touch Dis." While I was in Florida, before the departure to Madeira, I had the pleasure of visiting Merritt's yard and going through the Robinson's new boat. What a project! This boat would be the biggest and surely the top of the Merritt fleet. They arrived from the airport around ten a.m. and we were off fishin' on "Pride" almost immediately. I was introduced to everyone and readied the video camera for the day's fishing. We were trolling by mid morning when Tim shouted from the top of the tower, his station while the boat is fishing, that there was a big fish following the left bait. Tim turned the boat to try and enhance the fish to strike but to no avail. The day had a lot of action with five fish being raised but no hookups. The fish were shopping but not buying, that's fishing!

In the afternoon Roy's father, Al Merritt, the senior Merritt, not to be confused with Senor Merritt as if we were in Mexico, came up to the bridge where I was awaiting a hookup with the camera equipment. We talked for a long time, and it was a real experience listening to his stories of fishing and boat building. The best part was when a fish would come into the baits he would harass Terry, Rick, and Tim about why we weren't hooked up. "Where's your drop backs," "Reel up the one he's chasin'," "Speed the boat up," "Go straight" and on and on. The boys took it all in stride. Al was having the time of his life.

That evening we had another superb dinner on board "Horizons" with all the guests. Lots of talk of big fish and other places they'd been and would be going. The wine poured and stories continued to flow after I retired for the evening. My flight for home was very early the next morning.

Just off Madera Island

The fish count for the four and a half days I was in Madeira was as follows:

Wed. 7/12: My first half-day. "French Look" releases 750- pound blue marlin.

Thurs. 7/13: "Pride" weighs in 995-pound blue marlin, "Chunda" releases 650-pound blue marlin on 30-pound test line, "French Look" releases 360-pound blue marlin and Roddy Hayes releases 750-pound blue marlin.

Fri. 7/14: "Americana" releases 720-pound blue marlin, "French Look" weighs in 1,203-pound blue marlin, "Pride" releases 650-pound blue marlin, local boat releases 1,070-pound blue marlin ("Pride" was next to them when this happened).

Sat. 7/15: "Pride" releases 900-pound blue marlin, "Chunda" releases 700-pound blue marlin.

Sun. &/16: Roddy Hayes on "Margarita" releases 680-pound blue marlin.

In four and a half days there were twelve marlin fought, ten of them released, and two taken. The smallest fish was a "rat" at 360 pounds and the next smallest was 650 pounds. All of this just a few miles off of the island, in the lee, ten minutes from the harbor, in beautiful blue water that is five thousand feet deep! In fact all of "Pride's" fish were inside of a one-mile circle.

I hated to leave and wished there had been a newer camera to video all the seasons daily action. It is almost impossible to video and to drive the boat at the same time or be in the cockpit and video, although many have tried. There is no replacement for an experienced cameraman on the bridge. I needed to get home. Back to taking care of business and all those other things that you do when you're home.

On The Road Again

My flight home was a story in itself. I'd have done better going as baggage with Federal Express. Early in the morning of June 17, I flew from Madeira to Lisbon, Portugal, on TAP Airlines and the flight was fine. The next leg home was on Delta Airlines flight 97. I went through all the security checks and boarded the plane. I welcome all the security checks because it beats the alternative! After boarding the plane we sat on the tarmac for four hours while they replaced a faulty navigation system. The replacement system was not FAA approved so the flight could not go great circle route, the shortest distance to New York. The flight had to be lightened by removing people and cargo, and loaded with more fuel so the plane could make its new flight plan via England, Iceland, Greenland, and Canada to New York. The flight would be ten hours, four hours longer than the normal flight. After boarding the plane I arrived in New York fourteen hours later. In New York I ran to the last plane to Los Angeles, arriving home twenty-seven hours after departing Madeira. The fishing was great there, but not if I had to pull that flight plan each time! Well, at least my bags made it. As it turns out Delta sent me an apology letter. How nice!

Chapter 10

Home Sweet Home!

Southern Californians were still recuperating from the recent recession, heck, even both of their professional football teams hit the road. The Raiders went back to Oakland and the Rams to St. Louis. Well, the good news was we'd have the pick of any game we wanted on television, and no blackouts.

The boat shop was doing well without me but they took me back anyway. The fishing season in Southern California was coming up so, between jobs, I readied our 27-foot Phoenix "Ghost Rider." There were a lot of small things to do but basically the boat was ready to go. Linda and I made several weekend trips over to Catalina where she was able to swim, take a few short hikes ashore, and relax.

I fished a few days, before the first tournament in late August, with minimum success. It looked as though this season might be a late one. The first tournament was the Church Mouse Tournament out of Avalon, Catalina Island. As I've said before, this is a fun charity tournament.

Church Mouse '95

No, Church Mouse is not a children's story although this year's tournament had a Cinderella ending. Hollywood scriptwriters would be hard pressed to top this true story.

The tournament was held on August 28, and 29, at Avalon, Catalina Island, with the briefing held on Sunday August 27, at one of Avalon's finest dining establishments. After the meeting and a great Eric's burger on the pier, our team "Blues Bros" headed for the boat and a good night's sleep. This "Blues Bros" team consisted of owner Chris Kozaites, Bob Lienau III, owner of Big Fish Tackle, located on the corner of P.C.H. and Seal Beach Boulevard, in Seal Beach, Willie Baxendell from Surfside, California and myself.

Four-thirty a.m. comes early no matter what time you hit the hay but we were all up and off to San Clemente Island, and beyond, for the first day of fishing. The "Board" at Avalon showed only five fish caught and two fish released this season before the first day of the tournament. This let everyone know the fishing might be slow.

The morning off of San Clemente Island started with a vengeance, lots of bait in the water and all kinds of signs of life but no sleepers. In fact the only fin we sighted that day was a sunfish!

As the day slipped past, one boat, "Crow Fleet," radioed in that they were hooked-up at the Forty-three spot. That just so happens to be forty-three miles from Avalon but is named for the fathoms down and not the miles out. An hour later they called in that they had lost the fish when the double line broke. That was the only valid hook-up of the day. As time slipped by some boats radioed in that they would be pulling in to Mission Bay because they were so far south. We ended up in Avalon and after re-fueling had an early night.

Tuesday morning we went to the "Domes," off of San Clemente Island again, but as we searched the area we found none of the signs of life that we had seen the day before. We worked the area for a good part of the morning with no luck and eventually moved off towards the 289 spot. First thing in the morning "Tail Chaser" and "Reel Lady" hooked up at the 43 spot further south of our position. An hour later "Tail Chaser" radioed in that they had lost the fish. A short time later "Reel Lady" reported that they had boated their fish and were on their way to Avalon to weigh in the first, and possibly only, fish of the tournament. An hour later we spotted them heading towards Avalon and we heard their fish weighed in at 115 pounds. By now we had turned back towards San Clemente Island and eventually made a course change towards Avalon as time looked like it was running out.

At 1:45 we were "bit" and soon the fight was on. After backing down for about thirty minutes in three-foot chop and twenty knots of wind, we landed the fish. It was almost two-thirty by the time "Blues Bros" was under way for Avalon, twenty-seven miles upwind and upswell. We looked at our time and realized it was going to be a close call getting the fish in to the pier by the four o'clock deadline.

I radioed in our E.T.A. to be three fifty-six. The Church Mouse officials came back saying that we had to have the fish ON THE PIER by four o'clock! Our response was

Rosie Cadman, and Blues Bros team: Mike, Willy Baxender, Chris Kozaites, & Bobby Lienau

"We'll be in by three fifty-six!" Our crew left the isinglass rolled up for less windage, jettisoned all of our fresh water and emptied all three bait tanks of bait and water to lighten the boat for the run to Avalon. Chris even went down into the engine room to see if he could get a couple more R.P.M.s out of the engines. The natural six-seventy-one G.M. diesels have been run "full rack" since Chris purchased the boat in 1978 and she runs as clean as a gas engine. The wind was up to nineteen knots with a four-foot chop but we were moving towards Avalon at a solid twenty knots... and the bridge stayed relatively dry! As we neared the half way mark tournament officials radioed us for an updated E.T.A. My response again was "Three fifty-six!" A lot of the other tournament boats were cheering us on as we headed north, the race was definitely on. Soon we found smoother conditions as we neared the "Slide" area near Avalon and our speed increased ever so slightly.

One problem was that the tournament officials had asked everyone to slow down as they neared the "Lovers Cove" area because it was cruise ship day. We radioed in and requested that as soon as they had us in sight at Lovers Cove to guarantee us a weigh-in and we would slow down as they had requested. Our request was denied so we reported back that we would abide by all navigation rules but we would be "hammer down" until the breakwater at the south end of the harbor. Their response was "No problem, they would notify the shoreboats working the cruise ships of our situation."

"Blues Bros" turned the corner at Lovers Cove at three forty-five. We made the dock at the crane on the pier at Rosie's at three fifty-six. Roger Cadman helped us tie-up and hoist the fish onto the pier. A few minutes later Rosie pulled the lever on the scale and the fish weighed in at 144.5 pounds, "Blues Bros" had won the tournament! Needless to say the awards ceremony was a lot of fun and over $11,000.00 dollars was raised for various charities of Avalon!

The Masters, Gold Cup and Classic

This year I fished with a couple different friends in the next few tournaments and had a great time. One tournament was the light line Masters Tournament. I skippered Hal and Debbie Neibling's "Gamefisher" out of Long Beach. The anglers used only Dacron and linen line. We had shots at three fish with one hook up on 16-pound Dacron that did not stick. We also baited one sleeper with six-strand linen. Fun was had by all but we did not place.

Next was the Gold Cup that went any way but right. Our team on "Jersey Maid" did everything. We had a game plan, checked all the gear and re-rigged every piece of tackle we might use, but it just wasn't meant to be. We all had a great time but were unable to place.

For the last tournament, Roger Cadman's Classic Tournament, we took my boat and the boys from the shop. A couple of weeks before the Classic we closed the shop and headed out for a two-day fishing trip to the island. The boys from the shop consisted of Tim Cooper, Santos Malpica and me. We never fished together before and I figured that with my half-ass Spanglish (Spanish/English), Tim speaking no Spanish, Santos speaking little English, and only having one eye, this could prove to be quite a trip! As the day went we had little action and sighted just a few of sharks. As the afternoon progressed "Ghost Rider" was heading down the back of Catalina Island toward Avalon. The breeze was up to twenty-two knots and the seas were three to four feet.

We were four miles from Church Rock at the East End and the lee of the island. The right short rigger went off. We were "bit." I had Tim as the angler and had talked with Santos about running the boat, "Just keep it down swell." He replied "Si." Well, Tim had never caught a marlin and Santos was mixing up the shifters with the throttles, so it was getting a bit out of hand. Surprisingly, after a few minutes, when I had all the other rigs in, Santos was going down swell SLOWLY, Tim had the reel on top of the rod and we passed the marlin back (so he was in back of the boat, where he should have been, instead of in front it), It was all getting a little easier. Twenty minutes later I wired the fish. Tim took two great pictures of the covering board with the fish and part of my face in the corner of the photos. We actually tagged the fish before releasing him.

That night we went into Avalon for some chow, then up to the Chi Chi Club to play a little pool. Santos won all three games, I guess he doesn't have any problem with double vision.

The next day Tim spotted a sleeper and Santos found us a jumper but without any hookups. The boys had a great time fishing and after a couple more practice days I decided we'd enter the Classic Tournament out of Avalon. Another good friend Mike Iwakoshi rounded out our team.

The first morning of the tournament we ran to the back side of the island and after having the lines in for about fifteen minutes we had a zip on the right long rigger. Mike dropped a bait back and we ended up on a slow troll of the area, because a couple of other boats with sonar were working the same area. Ten minutes later we were "bit" and for a few minutes it appeared to be a nice sized fish. When it jumped we realized it was just a nice sized mako shark. We made short work of him and continued to troll. The rest of the tournament was intense with just a couple fish spotted. We did not place in this event, but we had a damn good time, winning the first tournament of the season but not placing in the remaining ones.

Chapter 11

Madeira Madness

The middle of September found the boat shop busy and, in the middle of all this, Mitch called to tell me that "Horizons" would be departing Madeira for Puerto Rico around the eighth of October. He wanted me in Madeira on the sixth and had already sent me a ticket (not with the previous carrier). This should be a fairly quick trip since we were not going all the way back to Florida. October fifth found me Lufthansa-ing my way to Frankfurt, with a change to TAP Airlines from there to Lisbon, then to Funchal, Madeira. After a twenty-four hour flight, including connections, I arrived in Madeira. Waiting at the Barrilihnos marina side open air restaurant, until three-beer-thirty for someone to pick me up, Mitch and friends arrived from dinner. The group of us closed the place that night and for some reason we felt a bit off of our game the next day.

The boats were ready to go. "Horizons" had gone to Teneriffe in the Canary Islands to refuel a couple of weeks ago. At sixty-four cents a gallon there was quite a savings when they took on 66,700 liters, or 55.5 metric tons, or 17,370 U.S. gallons, of diesel. For the trip back to Puerto Rico we had a new cook, Chad Golding from New Zealand, and another second engineer, Rob McFarlane from Australia. So the crew would be Mitch, Splitpin, Rob, Chad and myself. Of course Hoby, who now looked like a Giant football with legs was still our mascot. Laura was flying to Australia and Adrian was flying to Mexico, for well-deserved vacations. Mitch would soon follow Laura once we arrived in Puerto Rico. Captain Tim was to arrive on Sunday from the States and the "Tyson's Pride" would be heading back to Palma, Mallorca, for the Dock Express ship back to Ft. Lauderdale. The fishing had slowed down a few weeks earlier but a few fish were still being caught.

Splitting Up Your Engineer

As the season in Madeira progressed, Splitpin was needed for his engineering abilities on a few of the other boats. Apparently Split had helped the "Chunda" boys a few of times. At one point Stewart Campbell, who holds at least five world records, came by "Horizons" and shanghaied Split to go fish one day. Split was always busy fixing one

Mark James "Splitpin"

thing or another and rarely had any time to fish or, for that matter, take off at all. Stewart told Split as they headed out to the grounds that he would wire Split's fish when he caught one. Stewart is sixty-three and usually the angler. Well after a short period they were hooked up, and after a short fight the fish was near enough the boat to wire. And sure enough Stewart wired the fish that they subsequently released. Not only was Split impressed with the fact that they fish using the "bait and switch" method but that he had the famous Stewart Campbell release his fish! Later Split took a pair of gloves and sprayed them silver and presented these to Stewart in appreciation for wiring his fish. Split also told him, with Stewart's crew around, that if Split ever caught a grander that he'd have Stewart wire that fish. He said this all in fun, of course.

During September the Madeira tourist bureau planned the first annual, blue marlin tournament. This would be a tag and release tournament only, and any team would be disqualified if they killed a fish. Almost all of the boats fishing in Madeira would do the tournament, including "Pride," but neither Don nor any guests would be there for it. As it was, Split and a few of the crew off of "Horizons" went out as the anglers on "Pride." The morning of the tournament Split told Stewart Campbell that if he ever wired a grander for him, Split would give him a pair of "Golden Gloves". However the day was quite slow and everyone aboard had a feeling that they might get shut out when, at three minutes to stop fishing, a big fish came charging into the baits and they were hooked up. This fish was Split's and the battle was on.

Adrian, the steward aboard "Horizons" and master of the margarita had mixed a mean brew that day. He and other crewmembers from "Horizons" had been a sippin' all day while they fished aboard "Pride."

The fight lasted a couple hours and a few times the crew had a good look at the fish. Everyone thought it weighed in at 1,050 to 1,100 pounds. Split asked Captain Tim to call "Chunda" on the radio to see if Stewart would come out and wire Split's fish. "Chunda" had been in the harbor for a while after the stop fishing so this was very feasible since "Pride" was only a few minutes from the harbor. Stewart heard the call and answered "Pride" saying, "Tell Split I'm coming out for the "Golden Gloves." Mitch, on "Horizons," took the big inflatable over to "Chunda," picked up Stewart and off to "Pride" they went, arriving in less than ten minutes, ready to wire the fish. Shortly thereafter Stewart wired the fish and they had a successful tag and release. Oh, and yes "Tyson's Pride" had won the tournament with that tag and release of an estimated 1,070-pound blue marlin! The whole lot of them went into Barrilihnos that night and cleared the place out. It was time for a celebration. After I arrived Split told me that the only thing he was worried about was the fact that he had caught a bigger blue marlin than Don had ever caught (although Don has caught much larger black marlin in Australia). "I don't think it's a problem," I told Split, "But it wasn't my problem, ha ha!" He did not think that was funny. A few days after the tournament the trophy presentation was held. When Split went up to give a very proper Australian speech he presented Mr. Stewart Campbell with a pair of Golden gloves for wiring his Grander. This was met with a roar of applause and laughter from the crowd.

Shelby's Record

"Pride" had a good season catching and mostly releasing their fair share of granders. Oh yeah.... they also set a world record! On July 23, one guest, Shelby Rogers, was the angler on another spectacular Madeira day when they were bit by a very large fish. She

Shelby's Fish

fought that marlin until the sun was going over the yardarm. With the expertise of crew and angler she landed the blue marlin. Later that evening after dark, with a crowd gathered on the docks in Funchal yacht harbor, the fish was weighed in. Shelby with "Tyson's Pride" owner, crew, and other guests watched as the digital IGFA certified scale hit 1,059 pounds, a new women's eighty-pound world record!

One Big Fish

One story "Pride's" fishing mate, Rick Thistlewaite, told Splitpin was when he had seen the largest marlin he'd ever seen any where in the world, one day while out fishing on "Pride" in Madeira. The fish came up just under the baits, just rolled, took a look but didn't strike. A few of the other boats said the same thing, that the giant fish seemed to come up in back of the furthest baits and never did strike, just window shopping. Rick said, "It looked like it was from Jurassic Park."

Madeira does not seem overly anxious to have a larger charter fleet. With the difficulty of getting a boat there and the smallness of the marina I don't think it will bother them if a lot of boats do not come over to fish their waters. This could help conserve these monster fish of Madeira.

Back Across The Pond

Well, Sunday October 8th arrived and so did Captain Tim and one other crew. Before we could finish saying the hellos, they were on their way to Palma, Mallorca, with "Tyson's Pride." They had the first good southerly of the season to leave in, that would put the wind at their backs and, hopefully, give them a comfortable trip up to Gibraltar. We sorted and packed "Horizons" most of the day and eventually went ashore for a pre-departure dinner that night.

The next morning we had anchors to hoist, boats to store and a thousand little things to do before we could depart. By three in the afternoon we were under way on course for San Juan, Puerto Rico, 2,770 miles away. The large northerly swells that lifted and lowered us as we cleared the island made us realize that the summer of '95 was definitely over. The next few days the conditions were fairly flat but as soon as the first of a couple eastbound lows crossed above us we had a bit of bad weather off of the starboard bow. These northerly storms were well above us and fairly predictable so we knew our weather would be tolerable. The one concern was any late tropical activity, (hurricanes) to the south of us. We had a weather fax that gave us government weather information. We were also in daily contact through phone and fax with our private weather routing service, a great help on all of the trips. The one thing we could not do with "Horizons" was to out run any weather system. The best we could do would be to turn to try and avoid its path. We were constantly plotting all weather systems in the Atlantic within a thousand miles of us.

The new chef, I realized, was experimenting with his menu, using us as guinea pigs. Usually this would not be a problem. However in this case he tried to kill us a couple of times in a row. The third night out he cooked up a great fish dinner, except it was Cajun style and would have made the proudest Cajun connoisseur run for the water hose or the head. The next day at lunch we had a simple Caesar salad and my guess is the spice rack must have fallen on it! Well after this, we asked him to just make meals that HE'D eat. That evening we had lamb, potatoes and a vegetable, whew! Chad made some darn tasty meals throughout the remainder of the trip. "Keep it simple stupid" was a cliche that fit Chad's new and revised menu.

Australia's Great Barrier Reef
(The Land of Oz)

On both the trips over to Madeira and back to Puerto Rico, Mitch, Splitpin and I talked a lot of the Great Barrier Reef off Australia. Both Mitch and Splitpin had worked the reef on various boats from motherships to gameboats. They said although the reef is over 1,000 miles long, the big black marlin area is in the northern area of the reef. This area is just 150 miles long, running from Lizard Island in the north to Cairns in the south. A lot of anglers fly to Lizard Island where the mothership/gameboat programs will send in the gameboat to pick you up. If the boats are fishing towards the south you may have to

The late Michal James wiring a 950 LB Black Marlin

charter a seaplane from Cairns to get to the mothership. No Name Reef, the extreme north end and east of Lizard Island, is just one of the spots where the motherships will anchor over night. Running north from Cairns we have, in order: Linden Bank, Opal Reef North and South, St. Crispin, Agincourt Reefs No's 1-4, Escape, Anderson, Ruby, Pearl, Lena, Ribbon Reef #1 to Ribbon Reef #10, and No Name Reef. Number Five is a popular spot with Laurie Wright, who is one of the better-known gameboat Captains. I met Laurie and Julie Wright in Flamingo Bay, Costa Rica, in 1989 when they were running the 46' Merritt "French Look." I was the delivery captain on "Desperado," on her maiden trip around from the East Coast via the Panama Canal. Laurie is one of the top Captains on the reef and his boat, "Balek III," seems to always be on the fish.

With the fish moving, there are so many reefs where the motherships can anchor that they are able to follow the fish up and down the reef. The first motherships began operation in the early seventies. "Bali Hai," "South Pacific II," "Mantaray," "Mustique," "Deja Vue," "Laura J," and the two "Achilles" are just a few of the motherships on the reef. The rent's a bit high for some but between the fishing, diving, reef, mothership life, people, and the country, the trip is well worth all that it's said to be. The motherships stay the whole season and can usually re-provision at Cairns in the south, Cooktown in the north or Port Douglas midway between Cooktown and Cairns.

The National Parks and Wild Life Service regularly opens and closes different reef areas, in fact, they have a degree of how open or closed an area may be. They do this to let the reef life in each area rejuvenate. They also do not allow any mining, drilling, commercial spear fishing, or scuba spear fishing in order to protect the reef.

American George Bransford, on "Sea Baby," was one of the first to ever fish the reef. Captain Peter B. Wright runs "Duyfken" and has been fishing the reef since the first boats started doing so back in the sixties. You can regularly find the top Captains, mates, and anglers on the reef during the season, September through the end of November.

Sewn up baits such as rainbow runners and mackerel are used when trolling. Also live baiting with tuna works well, with baits averaging up to twelve pounds and sometimes bigger. Fishing here starts late and can go 'til dark or even later if there's a fish on.

My friend, Al Bento, fished the reef a few years ago and while they were on the mothership, the gameboat captain talked them into going for a swim. I guess it didn't take long for the groupers (which can get well over 150 pounds) to come up, nip em' on the butt and chase them out of the water. The Aussies had a good laugh on that one.

The fishing on the reef has been world famous for years. Even with all the foreign commercial fishing in the neighboring waters, the giant black marlin caught here seem to arrive every year on time and attract anglers from all over the world.

Of course one of the greatest mothership captains that ever lived, Mitch, is sadly missed each year on the reef while he runs the mothership and gameboat program for Don Tyson in such places as Madeira, Panama, Brazil, etc....

Finish With A Flurry

As "Horizons" continued across the Atlantic, towards Puerto Rico, the water temperature warmed up but the fishing stayed cold. With the exception of some large low pressure areas that crossed the Atlantic from west to east above us, giving us a bit of grief right in our face, the trip had gone smoothly until October 19. I noticed that the barometer started dropping early on the nineteenth. I logged these constant changes in and made Mitch aware of the situation. With both our weather fax and our weather routing service we kept our eyes open for any tropical storms. Our trip across was a little early yet for the end of hurricane season. When Mitch contacted our routing service we asked for special attention to the fast drop in the barometer. They returned a report saying there would be clouds and rain on our track but no significant weather. That evening we received a weather fax showing a low just below our position approximately three hundred miles at best.... our concern grew.

The next morning we had heavy rain that lasted on and off most of the day and into the night. The wind and seas were not bad and actually had gone down. On October 20 our report from the routing service said that our luck with the tropics being so quiet had run out, oh great! They added that tropical storm Sebastian had formed just below and in front of our position. Timing has not been my strong point lately! Basically this system formed in the last day and a half right in our area. The good news was that we would probably distance ourselves from it in the next day. Don't you just love that word "probably?" The next day October 21, the weather service contacted us to let us know that Sebastian had actually increased in size and in speed.

Oh! And of course its direction had been northwest, towards us, and not northeast. The storm's speed increase to eleven knots meant that the center was now less than two hundred miles from us, towards the south-southeast. The service also felt that the system would be slowing and turning towards the northeast, I was hoping they were right. That afternoon the swells started to increase in size and the rainsqualls increased in number, size and intensity. The wind was still only seventeen knots, except when it increased in the squalls. "Horizons" was only a day and a half from San Juan, Puerto Rico. This morning we went over Echo Bank and even the fish had high-tailed it out of town! Sebastian did head northeast and slowed down in speed but had actually increased in size and intensity. In the last twenty-four hours we had crossed over the top of the system. With its movement slowing and turning towards the northeast we had avoided a head on confrontation with it.

Sebastian was the same distance from us as it was yesterday, but it was now almost directly behind us instead of below us. The situation started to look better. The next day October 22, we were twenty-four hours from San Juan and had moved sixty-five miles further away from the storm. It had changed direction once more towards the west and again had increased in speed, size and intensity. It was following our track! The next morning we arrived and were med moored in San Juan by eight thirty in the morning. The storm had changed direction to the south west and was heading for St. Maarten in the Caribbean, that had been nearly destroyed in early September by hurricane Luis. On the twenty-fourth the storm's intensity dropped but the system was still heading for the islands in the area of St. Maarten. The system would eventually cross over the islands of Anguilla and St. Thomas, then cross the bottom of Puerto Rico as it completely dissipated.

Club Nautico

We arrived in San Juan, Puerto Rico, and moored at the Club Nautico. Split, Rob, and Chad prepared for the mini refit they were about to start. They had a little over a month to do six months worth of work before their next trip, which would find "Horizons" and "Pride" on another adventure to Pinas Bay, Panama. Tim would be bringing "Pride" down to rendezvous in Pinas Bay, Panama, with "Horizons." Amadeo and Adrian would be flying into San Juan in a couple days to help out with the workload for the next month on "Horizons."

Hoby was not a happy cat. She did not like all the work and noise but she'd get over it. Soon she'd be standing watch on the bridge with all the attention she could possibly muster. Mitch and I packed for our flight home.

Always after a long crossing we have an arrival dinner. This was no exception. The whole lot of us went off to dinner in Old San Juan.

With "Horizons" secure at Club Nautico in San Juan, Mitch and I flew to Los Angeles. Mitch was on his way to take a well-deserved vacation, home in Australia.

During the crossing I called Al Bento to see if we might be doing the Lahaina Tournament again this year. He said that due to problems with the boat and finances he wasn't going to be able to do the tournament this time. I told him that I'd be over to do a little fishing for a few days some time soon, hopefully before Christmas.

Chapter 12

Into The Thick of It

The shop was in its usual disorder but things were happening and jobs were getting done.

Although the local marlin season had slowed, with most boats going to Cabo and people back to work, my friend, Alan Schlange, who also makes great rods, had been fishing between Catalina and San Clemente Islands on "Brandy Wine" late into the season. Between catch and or release he had six fish in the last week of October.

With all that was happening the subject of going to Hawaii was the one thing that made Linda smile. After a short discussion, we decided to go.

Back at the shop, Tim just shook his head when I told him Linda and I we're off to Hawaii. He just said, "Maybe when you get back I might be able to take a week off." "Sure, sure," is all I could come up with. I guess I owed him big for looking after everything.

As it went, due to the busy holiday travel season, lack of flights, crowds, and of course the peak holiday prices, we didn't get over to Hawaii until after the first of the year. We headed to Maui for a little business before going to Molokai for a couple days of R&R, and then to Oahu to fish with Al.

A Day Off! Let's Go Fishin'!

Maui was busy, Molokai relaxing, but we were both ready to visit some old friends by the time we arrived in Honolulu. I had planned to fish with Al a couple of days while there but with storm warnings up we only managed to get in one day.

One evening, a group of us where upstairs at the Hawaii Yacht Club when Al told us the story of the fish he caught.

He began by talking about the haul out. "Alele II," his 35 foot Radon, had been in drydock for a month, getting a complete overhaul. New props, bottom paint, and a total paint job from the boottop to the top of the bridge, even new cabin windows. As soon as the boat was launched Al and Frenchy stocked the boat for a two-day "Holo Holo" (fun) fish trip to hopefully help pay for some of the refit.

Early the first morning they were off from the slip in the Alawai Marina, Oahu, for the fishing grounds off of the Lanai Island side of Molokai Island. The first day they spent on the Penguin Banks catching smaller "football shaped" ahi. The trades were blowing twenty knots and the seas in the Molokai Channel were eight feet. This made the crossing to the banks not so much fun, but as they neared the banks the conditions seemed to back off just slightly. The ahi bite went on for a couple of hours, even catching a few mahi-mahi and ono (wahoo), while "Alele II" worked the same area. Landing these fish was not difficult since they were fishing for "food" fish with larger Penn 130 rigs. Eventually they made their way towards the harbor at Haleolono, Molokai, where they anchored for the night. By the end of the day they had both side deck boxes almost filled.

Haleolono is a small deserted loading facility at the southwest end of Molokai Island. The surrounding area is totally uninhabited, unlike the main harbor on Molokai Island, Kaunakakai. The wharf at Kaunakakai sticks out from the island almost a mile, where one can usually find a boat to pull up and sidetie to. After a walk down the wharf and

Pau Hana Hotel, Molokai Island

another half a mile down the beach, a cool refreshment under the huge, one hundred year old banyan tree at the Pau Hana Hotel and Restaurant can only taste great. Also, from what I have heard, there's been more than one person who has awakened in the morning under that tree after an evening there.

Al and Frenchy sipped a couple of cool ones as they watched another magnificent Hawaiian sunset from the deck of "Alele II" at anchor in Haleholono Harbor. After the refit and a long day of fishing they both hit the hay early. Four a.m. the next morning they were heading for the backside of Molokai Island.

The tradewinds and the swell were pumping on the north shore when they rounded the southwestern tip of Molokai Island and Laau Point. They then headed up the coast past the old Sheraton Hotel, rounded the north western tip of the island at Ilio Point and changed course for the "NOAA" weather buoy five miles north east of where the missing "O" buoy used to be located. This put them outside of the Kalaupapa Peninsula on Molokai Island by ten miles. Early in the morning the channel is usually not bad, in fact, most of the channels in Hawaii are best when crossed early in the morning. Today, however, was looking as though it wouldn't be a whole lot of fun.

If you have never seen the north shore of Molokai, it is one of the most beautiful sights in the world. The island drops straight down for what seems like a mile, although it is not that far. The waterfalls with plush greenery are incredible and the way the ocean floor drops off, the fishing can be unbelievable. The swells and seas from the trade winds are also unbelievable, as

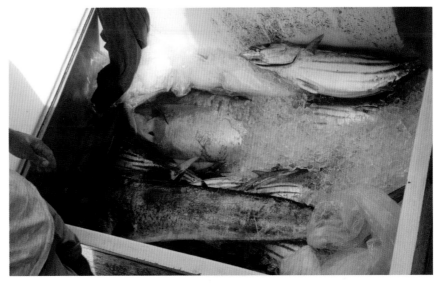

Alele II above deck fish box

was the case today. The trades were blowing a good twenty-five knots with the swells over ten feet, it could be worse.

Al and Frenchy had a good bite in the morning fishing for mahi mahi with live bait at the "NOA" buoy but, as the day progressed, the fishing backed off. Al had his two deck boxes full and the large center deck box, where the fighting chair usually goes, was maybe half full. The ice would keep the fish cold until he took them to market.

As the afternoon came on and as "Alele II" was getting abused from the large north swell and chop, Al decided to head on back to Honolulu. Fifty-one miles away, equivalent to over a five-hour run. Frenchy took the wheel while Al changed a couple lures from small kine to marlin kine. That Budweiser tasted good going down ol' Al's throat as he sat down after getting all in order for the trip back. The lures were running perfect and the wind and seas were at his back. He kept watching his favorite marlin lures, "ol' blue" on the long rigger and his newer addition, the "silver fox," on the short rigger as they swam and popped in the wake. The other lines had smaller lures for the food fish but he didn't notice them.

Fifteen minutes had passed while they settled in for the down hill slide through the notorious Molokai Channel back to Oahu when Al turned almost instinctively to check the lures. As he turned, he sensed that something was not right. He took a good look at "ol' blue" and then across at "silver fox." As he looked at "silver fox" he spotted a huge dark object in the large swell behind the lure. He thought, "It must be a whale,...no,...its not a friggin whale, its one humongous marlin!" The fish was hanging below, just sizing up the lure. Al told Frenchy that they have a taker comin' in the back door. Frenchy turned and didn't immediately see the fish. At that moment the marlin lit up and attacked the "silver fox".... The "fox" died. The marlin sucked that lure down and was on her way.

As the old 130 Penn went off like the noon whistle, the grandma of marlins started in her furious quest to throw the hook. She jumped completely out of the water five times in two or three minutes, and must have jumped a total of ten to twelve times before doing the half body lunges for another ten or so times. Al looked at the line peeling off the reel, and before he grabbed it he was screaming at Frenchy to slow the boat down.

There was no reason to hit the throttles to set the hook on this fish. The fish was hooked and she knew it. Al always sets his drags tight, so when he finally pulled the rod from the covering board the hook was set. It sure was convenient that the fighting chair was in Al's garage! Just for situations like this, without a chair, the angler could sit on the aft end of the large deck mounted fish box where there is a IGFA gimble on the back of the box for the rod butt.

While the boat was in refit, so was Al's fishing gear. Al had rebuilt all of his rods and reels, putting on all new Maxima Tournament Line.

Al was at least half spooled when he finally set the drag just a click more and as the slowing boat slipped down a wave he gave the pole a slight pull. The fish had slowed down. Frenchy was trying to keep the boat down swell because if they were to get in the trough in this, they'd be stuffed. Al could not believe his eyes as this monster jumped, all he said was, "It's a f@#!*!# boxcar!" They knew that the fish was big and they had their hands more than full. As all this was happening the wind was building with gusts over thirty knots. A lot of water was coming over the covering boards. Luckily most of it was going back out through the deck drains when they weren't under water themselves, both bilge pumps were on constantly.

 The fight went on for three hours and thirty-five minutes. The monster made a couple more runs, thankfully not far enough to spool Al or to out run "Alele II," although at one point there was less than 50 yards remaining on the reel, with more than 900 yards straight down. At this point things did not look good. The fishing line finally stopped paying out and Al was able to stop the beast. It soon became obvious to them that the fish had died.

They had to plane it up to the boat. It can take hours to get the fish to gaff. By slowly doing large oblong circles they raised the fish up to the surface, gaining small amounts of line at a time. When they finally gaffed it, both Al's and Frenchy's voices were hoarse. Even with a three to one block and tackle they were only able to get the eye of the fish even with the covering board (no marlin door) and onto the aft end of the boat. Over three-quarters of the fish was hanging over the transom and straight down into the water. As the sun was headin' for the land of the rising sun and the daylight dimmed they secured the fish best they could and headed off for Honolulu. The trip home was going to take a little longer than expected. Running at ten to twelve knots at night, with the fish hanging down in the water (not to mention the possibilities of a shark taking a little nibble out of the fish) Al and Frenchy were just a bit concerned.

In the middle of the night small boats with not much lighting and a large black object hanging off the back can be very suspicious anywhere, but especially when coming from the direction of the north shore of Molokai Island. It has somewhat of a reputation for its natural grown exports.

At 10:30 p.m. "Alele II" slipped past Diamond Head buoy and into the partial lee of the island of Oahu, you could not see the silhouette of the unlit 90-foot coast guard cutter sliding out to greet her. With a flick of a switch the blue lights and spot lights came on and trained on "Alele II." Over the loud hailer Al and Frenchy heard "This is the United States Coast Guard, heave to immediately and prepare to be boarded." As the cutter closed Al could see that the crew on deck were armed with what appeared to be AR-14's and sighting in on them. Al yelled with his hoarse voice, "What's up? We are trying to get to Hawaii Yacht Club to weigh in our fish!" The voice from the deck said, "What is the black object?" Al replied, "It's a marlin!" As the cutter came up almost on top of them someone from the bridge asked what Al had said. Al could hear a couple of wise cracks from the cutter, then the same voice asked the same question again, with the same reply from Al (plus a few expletives). The cutter captain asked what Al had said. The reply was "He said it's a marlin!" At almost the same time one spotlight lit up the back deck and the fish and almost simultaneously you could hear, "Holy Shit! It's a HUGE marlin!" from the crew on the deck. Al again requested that he be allowed to continue on his way to Hawaii Yacht Club. The cutter responded "All's clear, we'll escort you in!" This had been a long day, and it wasn't over yet.

"Alele II" pulled up to the Aloha dock at Hawaii Yacht Club and the few who were around could not believe the sight! Al called ahead on his cellular phone and had rounded up a group of people to help pull the fish from the water up onto the dock. It took a few good heaves by fifteen people to accomplish this task. With the fish completely laid out on the dock, it was the first time Al and Frenchy had seen the whole fish. They were amazed at its size! Al's first words were "My God, it's a monster!" A few minutes later the marlin was hauled up on to the lawn near the barbecue. The fish could not be weighed because the certified scale was locked in the yacht club office and there wouldn't be anyone with a key until morning, only a few hours away. The next step was to ice the fish down, and the one thing Hawaii Yacht Club does have, other than its hospitality and Aloha, is ice, plenty of ice.

In the morning the fish was moved to the scale area, and though most hadn't slept, the official weigh-in commenced. When the fish was hung up and the button was pushed on the certified digital scale, the fish weighed in at 1,207 pounds! There was a roar from the group that had gathered. After taking measurements and using the formula, it was figured that the fish probably would have weighed in at thirteen hundred and fifty plus, if it could have gotten to scale quicker; the fish was not weighed in until more than sixteen hours after it was caught. Al did not care, he was a happy Portugue'. As soon as all the pictures were taken and the crowd dispersed, the fish was cleaned and frozen. Al makes a mean smoked marlin.

Al was on cloud nine. He had just realized his dream. Lacking an unlimited checkbook it seemed an impossible accomplishment, and he did it in his own back yard. It goes to show you, you never know who's gonna get what, whether it's "Alele II" or "Tyson's Pride" that's fishing. Al now has a plaque onboard that someone gave him that says, "Oh great Kahuna, thank you for letting me catch a fish so big that even I don't have to lie about it!" The measurements for Al's Pacific blue marlin were, length 16'-4", dorsal girth 78", anal fin girth 76", tail girth 21.5". The time from boating the fish to weigh in was sixteen and a halfhours. This fish also qualified Al for the IGFA's Five to One Club, because the fish outweighed the tackle by more than five to one.

The marlin was the largest IGFA blue marlin caught in the world in 1994.

Sitting with us as Al told the story was Al's sweetheart Rhonda, Frenchy, Carl Myers, my brother Tom, a host of others and myself when Linda walked through the gate to the club. I went down to meet her.

Frenchy Luttgau, Al Bento & 1,207 Pacific Blue Marlin

Alele II

Well, let's celebrate! After the next round she handed me a letter from Mitch. Inside the letter was a copy of an old IGFA newsletter showing two giant marlin that were caught by net down in the south Pacific. One fish weighed in at 2,650 pounds without the internal organs. The other fish had not been weighed but was bigger than the first.

Jeff Silver, Al Bento, Mike Elias & Frenchy after a Grand Slam in Hawaii, 1993

Mitch proceeded to say that maybe after another season at Madeira, the "Horizons" program might go Tahiti way to look for one of these giant marlin to entertain the cockpit crew of the "Pride." He also said don't bet on it, but you never know!

Al, Mike, KeAlii & Alele II, 2000 Hanapa'a Tournament, Haleiwa, Hawaii

I read the letter aloud and as we all had a good laugh, someone asked, "What the hell would you call a marlin that big? A tonner? A giant? A monster?" Someone replied, "I guess whoever catches THAT marlin can call it what ever they damn well want to!" Then I turned to Al and said, "Ya know Al, (holding the newsletter) these fish were caught just a little south of here (2,500 miles!), I'd better give Mitch a call!"

MONSTER MARLIN *from the past. The photo of the Pacific marlin on the front end loader (right) was sent to IGFA by Herve Picarda, president of the Port Vila Game Fish Club in Vanuatu where the fish was caught but not weighed. Yves Guilbert of the Horea Royal Fishing Club in French Polynesia, sent the picture of the hanging blue marlin caught by Marii Terriipaia by commercial methods between Bora Bora and Tahaa. The fish was cut in half for weighing and totaled 2,650 lb, and this did not include internal organs. Both fish were caught in the 1970's. Terriipaia said he recently saw a marlin that was just as large. Another IGFA member sent in a newspaper clipping of a South Pacific blue marlin 19 feet long which was too big for the 880-pound scale.*

A Tonner? A Giant? A Monster?

These fish do exist. There have been other reports of marlin this big caught in nets and even by some long line boats. Commercial boats do not seem to want to let outsiders know of these catches, since they slaughter a good number of billfish each year. At Vitoria Yacht Club in Brazil there was a photo taped on the inside of a window that showed a marlin eighteen or nineteen feet long that could have gone over two grand easily. That fish was caught accidentally, in a net, by local fisherman.

A few years ago the "Chunda" group was in the Cape Verde Islands off the West Coast of Africa on a chartered Bertram 31. They had a huge blue marlin come in to the lures behind the boat. The fish was estimated to be over the 2,000-pound mark. They tried everything to hook up to this fish, but the marlin was only taking a look, and although

they eventually followed the fish for a while, they were unable to hook up.

A couple years ago my friend, Scott Lewis ("Chief / Vernski") was working in the Azores on "Double Header" when a giant blue marlin came in to the baits behind the boat. I remember him telling me about the incident. Scotty said, "Mike, I don't even want to tell you about this because it's hard to believe. Remember Mongo, well I met Mongo's mom! This 'slob' came in under the baits, she was minimum 2,500 if she was a pound! The marlin hung down under the baits for a while, but no matter what we did, we couldn't get her to hit anything!" He also mentioned that the "tater head" (charterer) thought it was a small whale. Scott is one of the most talented and experienced fishermen in the world.

I have met many owners, captains and crews who believe they will be the first to land one of these giants, a marlin over 2,000 pounds, that would be quite a record. These crews are ready for that shot.

It seems that marlin, especially the larger, older ones, are a lot smarter than people have given them credit for. In the last few years, the sightings of these giant marlin by reputable anglers in the area between the Cape Verde Islands and the Azores, with Madeira in the middle, seem to prove that this area has not been fished out or abused commercially. Government and anglers alike, by encouraging tag and release fishing, are helping preserve these marlin for future generations.

Epilogue

Years ago when I was just old enough to hold my pole, or a fishing pole for that matter, my father George C. Elias used to take me fishing. There seemed to be a lot more fish then. The stories he would tell me of fishing the Sea of Cortez in Mexico, with the likes of Ray Cannon and friends, didn't mean much to me then. The sights they must have seen and the fish they fought would be wonderful to experience today.

Seventy percent of the earth is covered by water. Respect your oceans and release your fish, treat all so future generations can enjoy.

During the '95 season I was having a conversation with Al Merritt on the bridge of "Tyson's Pride," in Madeira, when he told me that a lot of anglers don't release fish properly. He mentioned that any release fish should be handled with care, don't boat and then release just to get a good picture. Be careful when removing hooks, the less trauma the better. Always make sure your fish is revived and swimming before you release it. Good advice from an expert.

If you take a marlin, take care of it until it's weighed and cleaned. Pull the fish into the cockpit and place it in an insulated fish bag or cover it with towels and keep it wet. A swimstep marlin is a disgrace. Make sure the fish gets eaten and not wasted. If possible, of any species, only take what you are going to consume.

For the armchair angler, get off your butt and enjoy the oceans while you can, "someday" might have been yesterday!

Good fishing to you, enjoy it while you can!

Blue Marlin Madeira '95

About the Author

Michael J. Elias was born in 1951 in Los Angeles, California. His family had him onboard a boat before he could walk. His father George C. Elias was an avid fisherman. He would base the family in Avalon, Catalina Island on their boat for most of the summers when Mike and his brother Tom were growing up. He always seemed to be in some kind of mischief with his Islander friends Johnny Cadman, Joe Grey or Steve Crow. Mike always enjoyed fishing with his family, even after he caught his first mako shark at ten years of age. His family told him, "It could jump into the boat," as they went into the cabin and closed the door behind them. "I was a little concerned at that point," Mike later mentioned.

After living on a boat during his high school years Mike took up sailing. Between fishing, sailing and surfing he had little time for school but managed to graduate with a decent grade point average. He also did side work on various boats in the harbor to earn spending money. Mike surfed in the United States Surfing Championship in 1969. He also took well to Yacht racing. By his mid twenties he was crew aboard many world record long distance races. Later he would be the navigator on the "AIKANE X-5" when she set a new sailing world record for sailing from Los Angeles to Honolulu in 6 days 22 hours 41 minutes and 12 seconds.

"I never told my sailing friends about my fishing and also never told my fishing friends about my sailing." After a fifth time as a skipper in the prestigious Congressional Cup Match Racing Series Mike directed his attention to more serious fishing, mainly for the local marlin. "Southern California is not know for the size of the marlin but the techniques needed to be a productive marlin fisherman are amazing," says Mike, "I have seen some world class fishermen and deck hands come to southern California and just get frustrated. The guys that regularly catch and release marlin there are well tuned to the various methods needed to be successful."

After studying and passing his captains exam, Mike ventured into more lucrative yacht and small ship deliveries, taking him virtually all over the world. He was able to do a lot of fishing on most of the deliveries.

After marrying Linda in the early 80's Mike opened up a shipwright business in Long Beach and began taking on the jobs that most would not. "Most projects are very different and complicated; modification work is what I like most," Mike mentioned. So between fishing, some sailing, some surfing, married life, the "Shop" and a few deliveries he managed to write occasionally and eventually put this manuscript together. He still resides in Long Beach, California.

Glossary

Back down: running the boat in reverse to follow or chase a fish.

ballyhoo: type of bait fish.

bit: to be hooked up.

bit off: when a fish breaks the line.

the "Board" at Avalon: where the order of marlin catches and releases are listed each season.

covering boards: top outside edge of cockpit.

Cuba Libre: a type of cocktail, rum and cola with a lime.

down rigger: weights to troll deeper in the water.

drop backs: baits, usually live, that are dropped back into the wake when a marlin comes into the lures behind the boat.

feeders: marlin feeding on bait.

flat line: fishing line clipped on transom or coveringboard.

Gimbal: allows butt of rod to rotate while fighting a fish.

GPS system: navigation by satellites.

GRANDER: one big marlin, weighing over one thousand pounds.

Grand Slam: catching one of each main species in any given area, on the same day.

greyhounding: marlin doing a series of jumps in a straight line.

haole: basically, not a Hawaiian.

head: bathroom

holo holo trip: fun fishing trip, not a charter.

how nice: Screw you, (polite version)

IGFA: International Game Fish Association, Governing body of sport fishing

kine: Hawaiian slang for kind, type of item.

lit up: the bright iridescent colors the marlin changes to when excited.

longliner: commercial fishing vessel that sets lines that can be miles long.

med moored: a style of anchoring, anchor off of bow with stern tied to the dock.

outriggers: poles angled out from the sides of the boat used to spread out the lines being trolled behind the boat.

Perro: Spanish for dog, anti perro = cat.

poki: Hawaiian-style marinated raw fish.

quarter: pursuing a hooked fish that is forward of the beam of the boat.

Rhumline: direct course to a specific location

rigger clips: used to hold fishing line in outrigger so line will automatically release when fish strikes the lure.

rocket launcher: type of rod holder where rods are lined up in a row.

sewn bait: baits that are cleaned and sewn up to swim better while trolling, often frozen.

short corner: a style of trolling where bait is closer to the stern of the boat at one corner than at the other corner.

shot: a chance to hook a marlin.

sleepers: marlin sleeping on the surface, more than one can be in close proximity of another.

smoked a reel: during a hook up when the line is going out extremely fast and the reel fails.

soaking a bait: drift fishing with live bait.

"spit the dummy": Australia slang for "losing it", whether it be a temper or a fish.

stop fishing: in a fishing tournament, time previously set that the fishing lines must be reeled in for the day.

stuck: Aussie term for not happy, upset.

tail wrapped: fishing line wrapped around a fish tale.

tailer: marlin swimming down swell.

transom: back of boat.

unbuttoned: when a fish comes off the hook, not your shorts!

wanker: Aussie term for person who is a goof off, unreliable, dumb shit.

wire man: person who grabs the leader when tagging or gaffing a large fish.

wired: term used originally when the leader is in the wireman's hand, piano wire has been and still is used occasionally world wide for leader material.

zeppo: An endearing Aussie term for yanks.

zips: strikes on a lure or bait with no hook up.

Current World Records*

Line Class	Weight	Place	Date	Angler
Pacific Blue Marlin				
M-08 kg	204.11 kg	Milolii,	May 2, 1985	Martin G. Abel
16 lb	450 lb	Hawaii		
M-10 kg	348.67	Buena Vista,	Nov. 22, 1982	Eugene A. Nazarek
20 lb	768 lb 10 oz	Mexico		
M-15 kg	500.54 kg	Kailua, Kona	June 25, 1987	Kelly K. Everette
30 lb	1103 lb 8 oz	Hawaii		
M-24 kg	528.89 kg	Kailua, Kona	Aug. 19,1993	Ray G. Hawkes
50 lb	1166 lb	Hawaii		
M-37 kg	459.94 kg	Manta,	May 12, 1985	Jorge F. Jurado E.
80 lb	1014 lb	Ecuador		
M-60 kg	624.14 kg	Kaaiwi Point,	May 31, 1982	Jay Wm. De Beaubien
130 lb	1376 lb	Kona, Hawaii		
W-08 kg	287.01 kg	Pinas Bay,	May 8,1984	Linda L. Miller
16 lb	632 lb 12 oz	Panama		
W-10 kg	184.16 kg	Mazatlan,	May 18, 1972	Marguerite H. Barry
20 lb	406 lb	Mexico		
W-15 kg	289.84 kg	Kailua, Kona	Oct. 8, 1988	Jocelyn J. Everett
30 lb	639 lb	Hawaii		
W-24 kg	325.0 kg	Cape Karikari,	May 11, 1985	Irene Jamieson
50 lb	716 lb 7 oz	New Zealand		
W-37 kg	452.2 kg	Batemans Bay,	Mar. 14, 1999	Melaine Kisbee
80 lb	996 lb 14 oz	NSW Australia		
W-60 kg	430.92 kg	Le Morne,	Dec. 16, 1994	Maria Rosa Tomaini
130 lb	950 lb	Mauritius		
Swordfish				
M-08 kg	110.45 kg	Ft. Lauderdale	June 7, 1984	Robert Ray Goldsby
16 lb	243 lb 8 oz	Florida		
M-10 kg	140.61 kg	Palmilla,	May 24, 1979	David G. Nottage
20 lb	310 lb	Baja, Mexico		
M-15 kg	177.81 kg	Nantucket,	Aug. 3,1976	John F. Willits
30 lb	392 lb	Mass. USA		
M-24 kg	291.9 kg	Mercury Bay,	Apr. 2, 1998	Ian O'Brien
50 lb	643 lb	New Zealand		
M-37 kg	298.01 kg	Algarrobo,	Mar. 20, 1989	Fred Cameron
80 lb	657 lb	Chile		
M-60 kg	536.15 kg	Iquique,	May 17, 1953	Louis B. Marron
130 lb	1182 lb	Chile		
W-08 kg	78.92 kg	Pinas Bay,	Feb. 17, 1986	Deborah M. Dunaway
16 lb	174 lb	Panama		
W-10 kg	128.4 kg	Gordon's Bay,	May 4,1993	Marg Love
20 lb	283 lb	South Africa		
W-15 kg	135.80 kg	Hout Bay,	May 12,1995	Maureen K. Colyn
30 lb	297 lb 15 oz	South Africa		
W-24 kg	223.28 kg	Montauk Point,	July 4, 1959	Dorothea L. Cassullo
50 lb	492 lb 4 oz	New York		
W-37 kg	350.17 kg	Iquique,	June 7, 1954	Mrs. L. Marron
80 lb	772 lb	Chile		
W-60 kg	344.28 kg	Iquique,	June 30, 1952	Mrs. D. A. Allison
130 lb	759 lb	Chile		

*As of this printing